Sadie Blakesley

Paula,

Please read if you
will and return so
I can read it. The
lady at the book store
said she had been
having lots of questions
concerning Mary the Mother
of Jesus.

Love In Christ,
Sadie

D1412038

REFUTING THE ATTACK
ON MARY

Father Mateo

✝

REFUTING THE ATTACK ON MARY

A DEFENSE OF MARIAN DOCTRINES

CATHOLIC ANSWERS
SAN DIEGO
1999

Published by Catholic Answers, Inc.
2020 Gillespie Way
El Cajon, CA 92020

(888) 291-8000 (U.S. orders)
(619) 387-7200 (int'l. orders)
(619) 387-0042 (fax)
www.catholic.com (web)

Cover and interior design by Claudine Guerguerian
Printed in the United States of America
ISBN 1-888992-08-5

TO JOANNA WEIQIAO XIE

CONTENTS

FOREWORD

Among non-Catholics, in particular those styling themselves "Bible-believing Christians," the most misunderstood and disputed Catholic doctrines are often those concerning Mary. Catholics likely receive more questions about these doctrines than about any other Catholic beliefs.

Marian doctrines are often the target of non-Catholic organizations which profess to represent "orthodox Christianity" and to provide a proper understanding of the Bible, Christian history, and theology. In 1990, one such organization, the Christian Research Institute (CRI)—an Evangelical ministry headquartered in Southern California—published articles attacking Marian doctrines and Catholic veneration of Mary. The articles appeared in the group's magazine, the *Christian Research Journal*.

CRI, best known for its "Bible Answer Man" radio program, tried to give a definitive refutation of the Catholic position. In response, Catholic Answers asked Father Mateo to draft a critique of CRI's articles. The critique was serialized in Catholic Answers' monthly magazine, *This Rock*, over seven issues, from August 1992 through February 1993. Those serialized articles, slightly revised and supplemented, appear in these pages. The author wished to thank Elizabeth Hockel for her assistance in preparing the original typescript of the pieces.

Father Mateo was the pen name of a Catholic priest who was an emeritus professor of New Testament Greek at a prominent university. He spent nearly fifty years of his priesthood promoting the faith, especially among young people. Not content to work only in the classroom, from 1987 to his death in 1996, Father Mateo hosted the "Ask Father" forum on the Catholic Information Network (CIN), which began as a computer bulletin board system (BBS) and graduated to the World Wide Web (www.cin.org). Many of the answers he gave are still available online.

INTRODUCTION

By venerating the Mother of Jesus, Catholics are "injuring ecumenism." We are guilty of "scriptural blindness where Mary is concerned." We should realize that "idolatry is sin—and religious devotion to anyone but God is idolatry." Conclusion: Catholics are idolaters. So we are assured by "The Mary of Roman Catholicism," a two-part article published in the *Christian Research Journal*, the magazine of the late Walter Martin's Christian Research Institute.

The author of the article, Elliott Miller, is the editor of the *Journal* and is a top staffer at CRI. His views express the views of the organization, and he writes as CRI's spokesman. It is therefore fair to say the words of the article are the words of CRI. Throughout this and subsequent articles I will be referring to "CRI" as the responsible party.

Near the beginning of the Marian Year in 1987, Pope John Paul II, in his encyclical *Mother of the Redeemer* (*Redemptoris Mater*), asked all Christians, "Why should we not all together look to Mary as our common Mother, who prays for the unity of God's family?" Stung somehow by the Pope's friendly words and bothered by "a campaign to revive Marian devotion in the Church," CRI goes on the attack. "The time has come for a Protestant response. Just as surely as a man cannot 'take fire in his bosom, and his clothes not be burned' (Prov. 6:27), Catholics cannot renew their emphasis on Mary without injuring ecumenism."[1]

The suggestion is clear: Mary is a fire we are taking to our Catholic bosoms. The honor we pay her is idolatry, sin. We risk our own salvation and endanger ecumenism unless we stop "adoring" and "worshiping" her.[2]

Proverbs 6:27 seems important to CRI. It is quoted in the text of the article[3] and is used again as a callout on the next page, "so that he who runs may read" (Hab. 2:2). Before we accept Proverbs 6:27 as a scripture having to do with Mary, we should read it in its context. Proverbs 6:23–29 (RSV) reads:

"For the commandment is a lamp and the teaching a light, and the reproofs of discipline are the way of life, to preserve you from the evil woman, from the smooth tongue of the adventuress. Do not desire her beauty in your heart, and do not let her capture you with her eyelashes; for a harlot may be hired for a loaf of bread, but an adulteress stalks a man's very life. Can a man carry fire in his bosom and his clothes not be burned? Or can one walk upon hot coals and his feet not be scorched? So is he who goes in to his neighbor's wife; none who touches her will go unpunished." It is clear. To apply any part of this passage to the mother of Jesus is sacrilege, a serious abuse of God's holy Word. CRI insults and defames the one who is full of grace and blessed among women by applying to her a verse which the sacred writer uses of an adulteress and a prostitute.

CRI claims to give a "Protestant response." The implication is that it is giving *the* Protestant response. Few Protestants will want this article to be their voice. There is abundant evidence today of a growing interest in Mary among Protestants. The Protestant theologian K. E. Skydsgaard writes, "Mary's name shall not disappear in anonymity, but shall be recalled in every age and praised as holy. Evangelical Protestantism must also learn to sing this song."[4]

The German Evangelical *Adult Catechism* says, "Mary is not only Catholic, but she is also Evangelical. . . . Mary is clearly the mother of Jesus and closer to him than the closest disciples."[5] This new Protestant interest in Mary is more and more in harmony today with our Catholic devotion. By the power and will of her Son, which directs us all, she does seem to be drawing us closer together.

REFUTING THE ATTACK
ON MARY

1

DIVINE
MATERNITY

+

I shall follow CRI's order of topics in responding to its attack upon our Lady. The first objection is to our calling her "Mother of God." CRI asserts that the Church "officially assigned the title *theotokos* (Greek: God bearer or Mother of God) to Mary" at the Council of Chalcedon in A.D. 451.[6] Joseph Gallegos, a Catholic layman who frequently signs on to the Catholic Information Network, a computer bulletin board system, noted in one of his online letters that "[CRI] is twenty years too late. It was at the Council of Ephesus in A.D. 431 that *theotokos* was affirmed as a title of our Blessed Mother."[7] CRI makes this mistake four times within two pages.

CRI fears that the title "Mother of God," used "without strict qualification will naturally result in serious confusion, especially on the part of the theologically unschooled."[8] But the same is true of every other Christian doctrine. When worshipers sing the final verse of the grand, old Protestant hymn, "Holy, Holy, Holy," they segue into "God in three Persons, Blessed Trinity" and finish with a triumphant "Amen"—all without adding any "strict qualification." Yet if any doctrine needs careful explanation, the Trinity does. So we are bound to teach and explain every doctrine, but never to muffle or drop a single one.

Before his Incarnation and from eternity, the Word is God and pure spirit, as are the Father and the Holy Spirit. But in his Mother's womb he took human nature and became the God—Man, Jesus Christ. The titles "Mother of Jesus," "Mother of the Lord," and "Mother of Christ" can be correctly and devoutly used. But the history of doctrine shows that each of them has been misunderstood by some to suggest that Jesus was in some way less than God. Only "Mother of God" leaves the hearer in no doubt about Christian belief in his full divinity. Protestant theologian John de Satgé accepts *theotokos* and writes, "It is hard to see how any Christian theology can be genuinely evangelical without doing justice to it."[9]

Throughout his life Luther used and defended Mary's title "Mother of God" against all comers. "She is rightly called not only the mother of the man, but also the Mother of God. . . . It is certain that Mary is the Mother of the real and true God."[10] (I wonder about CRI's consistent failure throughout to mention *Protestant* sources in praise of Mary.)

CRI objects to the idea that "because of her divine maternity, Mary transcended all other created beings and stood next to her exalted Son in heavenly glory."[11] We do indeed believe that she is so exalted, partly because the Bible says so (Luke 1:42, 48; Rev. 12:1). But so do many Protestants of impeccable credentials.

Heinrich Bullinger, Cranmer's brother-in-law and Zwingli's successor, wrote, "She can hardly be compared with any of the other saints, but should by rights be elevated above all of them."[12] Drelincourt wrote: "We do not simply believe that God has favored the holy and blessed Virgin more than all the Patriarchs and the Prophets, but also that he has exalted her above all Seraphim . . . . the holy Virgin is not only the servant and the creature, but also the Mother of this great and living God."[13]

CRI asserts that Catholics exalt Mary above all other creatures simply because of her *physical* relationship to Jesus, whereas she is "blessed among women" (Luke 1:42) more because of her *role* in giving birth to the Messiah than because of the mere fact of her physical relationship to him.[14] But there is nothing in Holy Scripture to support *two* motherhoods in Mary, one purely physical, the other spiritual. In the real order, these cannot be and never were separated. She is related as a person to the person of God the Son. From her flesh she gave him flesh. Mary was not an incubator. She was and is his Mother.

Martin Luther said "God is born. . . . the child who drinks his Mother's milk is eternal; he existed before the world's beginning and he created heaven and earth. . . . these two natures are so united that there is only one God and Lord, that Mary suckles God with her breasts, bathes God, rocks him, and carries him."[15]

Mary is exalted above all angels and saints because God chose and prepared her, filled her with his grace to be his Mother. He drew from her freedom, by the premotion of grace, the full *Fiat* by which he accomplished the Incarnation. Christians who have not forgotten how to call her blessed know this well. "Men have crowded all her glory into a single phrase: the Mother of God. No one can say anything greater of her, though he had as many tongues as there are leaves on the trees" (Martin Luther, *Commentary on the Magnificat*).

2

PERPETUAL VIRGINITY

✝

By Mary's perpetual virginity we mean that she was a virgin before, during, and after the birth of her Son and for the rest of her life. CRI notes that this doctrine was "a subject of intense debate as late as the fourth century."[16] It alleges that "belief in Mary's perpetual virginity eventually won out thanks to the rise of asceticism and monasticism."[17]

CRI is in error here. There is no evidence whatever for this opinion. Anthologies of patristic spirituality prove that Jesus Christ, not Mary, was the ideal of virginity held up to monks and nuns from the beginning. John Cassian in his treatise *On the Eight Vices* (A.D. 425) writes, "If we are really eager . . . to struggle lawfully and to be crowned (2 Tim. 2:5) for overcoming the impure spirit of unchastity, we should not trust in our own strength, but in the help of our Master, God." The earliest accounts of monks and their lifestyle—like Athanasius' life of Anthony and Benedict's rule—give us Jesus, not Mary, as the monastic exemplar. It is the same with religious rules in later centuries. For example, the Thirty-First Congregation of the Jesuit Order (1965) declares, "The profession of chastity for the sake of the kingdom of heaven . . . shows wonderfully at work in the Church the surpassing greatness of the force of Christ the King and the boundless power of the Holy Spirit."[18] Certainly, Mary is important to all Catholics and in particular to those "who follow the Lamb wherever he goes, for they are virgins" (Rev. 14:4). It is ironic that, in its zeal to attack our Lady, CRI gives her more credit as a spark plug for monasticism than Catholics do.

CRI confuses things further by raising a triad of questions which are irrelevant to the issue of Mary's perpetual virginity:

1. Is celibacy a higher state than marriage?

2. Is asceticism a biblical tradition?

3. Does the gospel teach celibacy?

CRI answers "no" to all these questions, thus exemplifying what Max Thurian, when still a Calvinist, called "the anti-ascetic or anti-monastic reaction found in a certain type of Protestantism."[19]

Paul writes that "those who belong to Christ Jesus have crucified the flesh with its passions and desires" (Gal. 5:24). Our Lord teaches us that, to be his disciples, we must take up our cross every day (Luke 9:23). We hear him telling a would-be disciple that the Son of Man had nowhere to lay his head (Matt. 8:20), thus promising the man a lifetime of insecurity and discomfort. Elijah in the

Old Testament (1 Kgs. 17:1–7) and John the Baptist in the New (Matt. 3:4) are examples of an ascetical lifestyle. Even a cursory reading of the New Testament proves asceticism as Christian and, to some degree, a means to salvation.[20]

What about celibacy in the Bible? Elijah, Elisha, John the Baptist, Jesus, and Paul—these are examples of celibacy no Christian should undervalue. Jesus said, "Truly, I say to you, there is no one who has left house or wife or brothers or parents or children for the sake of the Kingdom of God, who will not receive manifold more in this time, and in the age to come eternal life" (Luke 18:29–30). With a flash of that rigorous honesty that often makes us wince, Jesus teaches us that "not all can accept this word, but only those to whom it is granted. Some are incapable of marriage because they were born so; some, because they were made so by others; some, because they have renounced marriage for the sake of the kingdom of heaven. Whoever can accept this ought to accept it" (Matt. 19:11–12).

But does the Bible's teaching on asceticism and celibacy diminish marriage? Specifically, does Mary's vocation to perpetual virginity imply disrespect toward her own marriage? No. Catholics regard marriage as a lofty vocation, elevated by Christ to the dignity of a sacrament of the New Covenant (Mark 14:4–9, John 2:1–10). Indeed, the indestructible bond between husband and wife is so awesomely holy that it is comparable only to the bond which unites Christ our Head to his Body the

Church (Eph. 5:23–32).

Now we turn to CRI's specific objections to Mary's life-long virginity. Elliott Miller asserts that Mary and Joseph had normal marital relations after the birth of Jesus, adducing as proofs Matthew 1:18 (*"before* they lived together, she was found with child") and 1:25 ("he had no relations with her *until* she bore a son").[21] These texts do not support CRI's contention. In Greek, *prin* ("before") and *heos* ("until") do not imply a reversal of situation upon completion of the "before/until" clause. Notice these examples:

1. "Come down before my child dies" (John 4:49)— yet the child did not die even after Jesus came down.
2. "Until I arrive, attend to reading, exhortation, and teaching" (1 Tim. 4:13)—but Timothy did not give up these activities after Paul arrived. Other non-inferential "until" texts the reader may wish to examine are Romans 8:22, 1 Corinthians 15:25, Ephesians 4:13, 1 Timothy 6:14, and Revelation 2:25–26. In short, Matthew 1:18 and 1:25 prove *nothing* against Mary's perpetual virginity.

CRI then refers to 1 Corinthians 7:3–5, asserting that normal marital relations were "in keeping with God's will for the couple."[22] I wonder how the writer knows precisely what was or was not in keeping with God's will for the couple. Later in the article we read, "While God certainly will do what is proper, theologians who take this approach to doctrine overlook the fact that they are assuming *a priori* that they know what is proper to God. Isaiah 55:8–9 tells us that God's thoughts and ways are not the thoughts and ways of man. This is true because God is not bound by the limitations of a finite nature and also because man's reasoning process has been distorted by sin."[23] Which is it, CRI? You can't have it both ways.

There is no evidence that Paul had Mary and Joseph in mind when he wrote 1 Corinthians 7:3–5. Moreover, Paul permits abstention from marital rights by mutual consent in 7:5. He wishes this to be temporary "so that Satan may not tempt you through your lack of self-control." This proviso could never have applied to Mary and Joseph. Furthermore, Paul recognizes the existence of particular charisms both within and outside of marriage (7:7). Certainly, perpetual virginity with abstention on the part of husband and wife is such a particular charism. The Pauline text, therefore, does not disprove Mary's perpetual virginity.

Now CRI comes to the often-urged question of the "brothers and sisters of Jesus" (Matt. 13:55–56, Mark 6:3, and elsewhere). The procedure used here is to attack Karl Keating, whose treatment of this vexed problem is now the best in the field of popular apologetics.[24] Keating needs no defense. His book is easily available to the interested reader. Here I want only to make a few observations.

The point at issue in the "brothers/sisters of Jesus" texts is the translation of the Greek words *adelphos* (brother) and *adelphe* (sister). CRI admits that the Greek Septuagint[25] uses these words not only for brother/sister, but also for remoter relatives.[26] Keating rightly notes that New Testament writers follow this Septuagint usage. CRI tries to dismiss Keating's argument with two counter-assertions:

1. "He never gives an example of a New Testament writer using *adelphos* for a cousin. . . . *There are no such examples*."[27] This is a red herring. Keating does not claim *adelphos* means cousin. He claims, rightly, that it often is used for "relative." And there *are* New Testament texts, which must be so translated. I invite the reader to examine Matthew 27:56, Mark 15:40, and John 19:25. In these James and Joses (Joseph), who are mentioned in Matthew 13:55 with Simon and Judas (Jude) as Jesus' *adelphoi*, are called sons of Mary, wife of Clopas, a different Mary from our Blessed Mother. This "other" Mary (Matt. 27:61, 28:1) is called our Lady's *adelphe* in John 19:25. It is wholly unlikely that two daughters of the same parents were given the same name, "Mary." Our Lady and the "other Mary" were related only in the wider sense of *adelphe*. They were relatives, but not sisters. Since Matthew 13:55 and Mark 6:3 mention Simon, Judas, and the sisters of Jesus along with James and Joses, calling them all *adelphoi* (masculine) and *adelphai* (feminine), these words in the

texts at issue must be translated "relatives."

2. CRI asserts against Keating that "The Septuagint is a translation of the *Hebrew* Scriptures and thus is not in a class with the *contemporary* narratives and letters of the New Testament."[28] But Septuagint usage is indeed a safe and necessary guide in interpreting New Testament Greek. From the middle of the second century B.C., many Jews in Egypt (where the Septuagint translation was made) and throughout the Diaspora had lost touch with Hebrew. The Septuagint began to be read in synagogue worship. By the time of Christ, for most Jews, the Septuagint *was* the Bible, their only readable Bible. This became true also for several generations of early Christians. Thus the influence of the Septuagint on the Greek language, as spoken and written by early Christians and by the Jews of the Diaspora and even in Palestine, was enormous. Almost 80 percent of the Old Testament citations and allusions in the New Testament come from the Septuagint, not from the Hebrew Bible. Stylistically, much of the New Testament, especially the four Gospels and Acts, is heavily dependent on the Septuagint.

David Hill of the University of Sheffield says, "The *vocabularies* [emphasis mine] of the Greek Old Testament and the Greek New Testament have a great measure of similarity; and research into the syntax of the Greek of the

Septuagint has revealed its remarkable likeness to that of the New Testament. . . . The language of the New Testament. . . reveals in its syntax and . . . in its *vocabulary* [emphasis Hill's] a strong Semitic cast, due in large measure to its indebtedness to the Jewish biblical Greek of the Septuagint."[29]

A. T. Robertson, in his *Grammar of the Greek New Testament in the Light of Historical Research* (1934), makes this remark about the nineteenth-century New Testament lexicographer and grammarian Gustav Adolf Deissman: "He properly condemns the too frequent isolation of the New Testament Greek from the so-called 'profane Greek' . . . he insists on the practical identity of biblical with the contemporary later Greek of the popular style."

The writers (except for Luke) and the very early readers of the New Testament, being Jews of that period, were "Septuagint conditioned." They were accustomed to the Septuagint usage of *adelphos/adelphe* as the ordinary Greek rendering of the Hebrew word *ach* in all its familial and extra—familial meanings, meanings much broader than uterine brother/sisterhood. Texts which call James, Joses, Simon, Judas, and the unnamed women the *adelphoi* and *adelphai* of Jesus cannot be understood except by calling these people Jesus' relatives, not his uterine brothers and sisters.

CRI, in fact, has ignored the historical and etymological importance of the Septuagint. It is as impossible to understand New Testament Greek without reference to the Greek of the Septuagint as it is impossible to understand the peculiarities of the Septuagint without reference to the original Hebrew.

CRI's next problem is with the Catholic interpretation of Luke 1:26–35. There, Luke says that Mary was a virgin and already engaged to marry Joseph when the angel Gabriel came to her. After greeting her, he calmed her fear: "Do not be afraid, Mary. You have found favor with God. You will conceive and bear a son, Jesus." Mary answered, "How shall this be? I do not know man" (a Hebraism for sexual intercourse). Her question shows that Mary knew how babies are made. The question makes no sense unless she resolved to remain a virgin even in marriage. Only then could she wonder how Gabriel's invitation could square with her resolve. When assured that her motherhood would not involve Joseph, but be altogether from the Holy Spirit, she acceded to God's plan as the "handmaiden of the Lord."

CRI attempts to refute the Catholic position by pouring contempt on the notion of a "vow of lifelong virginity, even in marriage."[30] Such a vow would be "unheard of and unthinkable in biblical culture"[31]—a statement unsupported by any kind of proof. CRI's phrase "biblical culture" is an abstraction so diffuse as to be nearly meaningless.

Besides, the problem here is not cultural, but theological. We are considering the Incarnation, and the Incarnation was unheard of and unthinkable in *any* culture. No human culture, "biblical" or not, could possibly anticipate or frame any detail of an event so shatteringly unique as the Incarnation of the Son of God. An integral part of God's plan for the Incarnation was the sole and total dedication of Mary to God the Son whom she bore in her womb and to the Holy Spirit, who possessed her utterly.

In 1 Corinthians 7:25–40 Paul bases his doctrine of marriage and virginity not on an appeal to prevailing cultural norms, but on his own apostolic authority (v. 25). His recommendations on virginity are in some ways "alien to biblical culture"—and to secular culture as well! He realizes this (v. 40a), yet insists on his decision in this matter, and he further insists: "I, too, have the Spirit of God" (v. 40b). To balk at Mary's vow is to nurse a non-problem. A vow is simply a promise to God to follow a course more excellent than its contrary. Mary did this. The conditions of a vow of virginity are perfectly met in her, as early and unbroken Church teaching affirms. Augustine made a very incisive remark on this subject: "Surely, she would not say, 'How shall this be?' unless she had already vowed herself to God as a virgin. . . . If she intended to have intercourse, she wouldn't have asked this question!"[32]

Several times CRI claims to present "the Protestant position" or "the Protestant view" or "a Protestant response." Yet Mary's lifelong virginity is well attested in Protestant sources too—something CRI does not mention. Martin Luther said, "Christ our Savior was the real and natural fruit of Mary's virginal womb. . . . This was without the cooperation of a man, *and she remained a virgin after that.*"[33] John Calvin also defended Mary's perpetual virginity: "Helvidius [a fourth-century heretic] has shown himself too ignorant, in saying that Mary had several sons, because mention is made in some passages of the brothers of Christ."[34] (Bernard Leeming reports that Calvin translates *adelphoi* as "cousins" or "relatives."[35]) The Swiss reformer Ulrich Zwingli wrote, "I firmly believe according to the words of the Gospel that a pure virgin brought forth for us the Son of God *and remained a virgin pure and intact in childbirth and also after the birth, for all eternity.* I firmly trust that she has been exalted by God to eternal joy above all creatures, both the blessed and the angels."[36]

John de Satgé says "There is certainly nothing in the Scriptures to invalidate the conclusion of the Church, in the days before the split between East and West, that Mary was a virgin all her life. . . . The full glory [of perpetual virginity] may be seen in the person of our Lord and his universal love, which all could claim and receive, but none could monopolize. In this sphere of *love's freedom* [emphasis mine] Mary enjoys to the full an identification with him. It has set her free for universal ministry."[37]

3

IMMACULATE CONCEPTION

+

CRI quotes Pope Pius IX in the official definition of the Immaculate Conception: "We declare, pronounce, and define that the doctrine, which holds that the most Blessed Virgin Mary in the first instant of her conception, by a singular grace and privilege granted by Almighty God, in view of the merits of Jesus Christ, the Savior of the human race, was preserved free from all stain of original sin, is a doctrine revealed by God and therefore to be believed firmly and constantly by all the faithful."[38] This definition of 1854 came after centuries of widespread Christian belief, meditation on Scripture, theological debate, liturgical development, and prayer.

In Luke 1:28, the angel Gabriel calls Mary *kecharitomene*, "graced," "endowed with grace." Jerome, in translating this Greek word, uses the Latin circumlocution *gratia plena*, "full of grace." CRI accuses Jerome of mistranslation and tries to refute Karl Keating's explanation of the original *kecharitomene*.[39]

Keating writes: "This grace . . . is at once permanent and of a singular kind. The Greek indicates a perfection of grace. A perfection must be perfect not only intensively, but extensively. The grace Mary enjoyed must not only have been as 'full' or strong or complete as possible at any given time, but it must have extended over the whole of her life, from conception. That is, she must have been in a state of sanctifying grace from the first moment of her existence to have been called 'full of grace' or to have been filled with divine favor in a singular way. This is just what the doctrine of the Immaculate Conception holds."[40]

CRI's objection is brief and rests upon one text, Ephesians 1:6: "Keating is reading more into the participle *kecharitomene* (derived from the verb *charitoo*) than its scanty New Testament usage allows. *Charitoo* is used of believers in Ephesians 1:6 without implying sinless perfection."[41] This is true, but CRI's next statement is false: "There is hence *nothing about Luke 1:28* that establishes the doctrine of the Immaculate Conception" [emphasis mine].[42]

The verb in Ephesians 1:6 does not imply sinless perfection, but the form of the same verb in Luke 1:28 does, because the two verb forms use *different stems*. Every Greek verb has up to nine distinct stems, each expressing a different modality of the verb's lexical meanings.[43] Ephesians 1:6 uses the first aorist active indicative form, *echaritosen*, "he graced, bestowed grace." This form, based on an aorist stem, expresses momentary action,[44] action simply brought to pass.[45] It cannot express any fullness of bestowing because "the aorist tense . . . does not show . . . completion with permanent result."[46]

But Luke 1:28 uses the perfect passive participle, *kecharitomene*. The perfect stem of a Greek verb denotes "continuance of a completed action";[47] "completed action with permanent result is denoted by the perfect stem."[48] On morphological grounds, therefore, it is correct to paraphrase *kecharitomene* as "completely, perfectly, enduringly endowed with grace." This becomes clearer when we examine other New Testament examples of verbs in the perfect tense:[49]

1. "*He has defiled* this sacred place" (Acts 21:28)—their entrance in the past produced defilement as a lasting effect.
2. "The son of the slave woman *was born* according to the flesh" (Gal. 4:23)—the perfect with reference to an Old Testament event can mean it retains its exemplary effect.
3. "*Have I not seen* Jesus our Lord?" (1 Cor. 9:1, Acts 22:15)—that Paul has seen the Lord is what establishes him permanently as an apostle.

Here, somewhat arbitrarily, are other examples I found:

1. "*God spoke* to Moses" (John 9:29)—the Pharisees hold that the Mosaic Law still and always holds.
2. "*It is finished*" (John 19:30)—the work of redemption culminating in the passion and death of

Christ is complete and forever enduring.

3. "He *rose* on the third day" (1Cor. 15:4)—unlike Lazarus who was raised from the dead but must die again, Christ rose to everlasting life.

4. "All things *have been created* through him and for him" (Col. 1:16)—all creation continually exists, upheld by God (this is the teaching of God's universal providence and also the refutation of deism).

Here are examples, like *kecharitomene*, of perfect participles in the New Testament:

1. "To the praise of his glorious grace, which he bestowed on us in his *beloved*" (Eph. 1:6)—Christ is perfectly, completely, endlessly loved by his Father.

2. "*Blessed* is the fruit of your womb" (Luke 1:42)—Christ is perfectly and endlessly blessed by God.

Because Luke 1:28 uses the perfect participle *kecharitomene* to describe Mary, CRI is wrong to say there is *nothing* in this verse to establish the doctrine of the Immaculate Conception. One word of one Bible verse does not *prove* the doctrine, but *kecharitomene* proves the *harmony* of the doctrine with Scripture.

CRI, you will remember, accuses Jerome of mistranslating *kecharitomene* with *gratia plena*, "full of grace." This is not nitpicking on CRI's part, and for two reasons: The phrase "full of grace" has guided many centuries of Catholic theological thought since Jerome, and some modern Catholic writers are of the opinion that *gratia plena* is a mistranslation. Against these Catholics and CRI, I contend that *gratia plena* is not at all a mistranslation. It is a felicitous phrase, as close to the Greek as Latin can come and much to be preferred to modern efforts to improve it: "favored one" (NAB [1986], RSV), "highly favored" (NIV), and the monstrosity, "highly favored daughter" (NAB [1970]).

Latin, when compared to Greek, seems to be an extremely awkward language. It is word-poor and has suffered considerable form-erosion. Specifically here, Latin has no verb that means what *charitoo* does in Greek. But using the resources that Latin does have, Jerome expresses the root meaning of *charitoo* by the Latin noun *gratia* ("grace," "favor") and the amplitude and completeness of the Greek perfect tense by the Latin adjective *plena* ("full"). The Latin phrase does not well connote permanent condition, as the Greek perfect participle does.

Catholics are not alone in this reading of *kecharitomene*. In his *Personal Prayer Book* (1522), Luther wrote, "She is full of grace, proclaimed to be entirely without sin. . . . God's grace fills her with everything good and makes her devoid of all evil. . . . God is with her, meaning that all she did or left undone is divine and the action of God in her. Moreover, God guarded and protected her from all that might be hurtful to her."[50]

Max Thurian, while still Protestant, wrote, "In regard

to the Marian doctrine of the Reformers, we have already seen how unanimous they are in all that concerns Mary's holiness and perpetual virginity. Whatever the theological position which we may hold today in regard to the Immaculate Conception and Assumption of Mary, . . . these two Catholic dogmas were accepted by certain Reformers, not of course in their present form, but certainly in the form that was current in their day."[51]

CRI says, "By virtue of his divine nature and his virgin birth (through which God, rather than a son of Adam, was his Father), Christ dwelt among us as One free from sin. . . ."[52] The implication is that Christ is sinless *partly* because he had no human father, no (sinful) son of Adam in his lineage. Given this premise one might think CRI should conclude that the Immaculate Conception is *necessary*: How could he be untouched by sin who would draw his human nature from a sinful mother? But this would be bad theology. The true reason for Christ's freedom from sin is the hypostatic union, which he shares with *no other human being*. Christ unites two natures, the divine and the human, in one divine Person.

It is this union which makes him, in CRI's words, "the *only* human who perfectly represents the holy character of the Father,"[53] "the refulgence of his glory, the very imprint of his being" (Heb. 1:3), "for in him dwells the whole fullness of the Deity bodily" (Col. 2:9). The hypostatic union anoints Jesus as our unique Messiah and Savior, our prophet, king, and priest, for the fullness of deity, which dwells in Jesus, dwells there for us: "Of his fullness we have all received" (John 1:16); "you share in this fullness in him, who is the head" (Col. 2:10).

Thurian wrote, before his conversion to the Catholic faith, "In Christ the Beloved . . . we are filled with the grace of God. . . . Mary, thus receiving the title of 'full of grace,' is at the same time placed in a privileged relationship of sharing in his fullness of grace, which is found in the Beloved, and united with all Christians, who can also find in Christ this same fullness. However, Mary receives this state as a title: That is to say, she becomes, as it were, a living and sure sign of this fullness of grace, which has its origin only in Christ himself."[54]

In conclusion CRI quotes Romans 11:32, "God has imprisoned all in disobedience that he might have mercy on all," and avers that the doctrine of the Immaculate Conception violates this "basic biblical principle." In fact, we are told: "To suggest that even one other person besides Christ was born [sic] without sin is to diminish the tremendous significance of the Incarnation."[55] Aside from the fact that CRI forgets about Adam and Eve, who were created sinless and lived the first part of their lives sinlessly (Gen. 1:31), CRI's argument does not follow, for two reasons.

First, Mary is not sinless by her own power, virtue, or merit. It was not her merits but those of her Son which were applied to her at her conception. The primacy and necessity of the Incarnation and Christ's fullness are not diminished by Mary's Immaculate Conception, because more than any other human being, she received of his fullness (John 1:16).

Second, as a child of Adam and Eve, Mary shares our fallen condition *de jure*. But *de facto* she was rescued from it at her conception. All was grace, but in her grace was preventive medicine. For us it is therapeutic, healing the actual damage of sin. CRI's proof texts (*dis*proof texts?) do not disprove the Immaculate Conception.[56] Mary's perfect fullness of grace was in God's plan necessary to what the Protestant theologian de Satgé calls "the awesome demands of her particular motherhood, without detaching that perfection from the grace that came by her Son."[57]

4

ASSUMPTION
OF MARY

✝

On November 1, 1950, Pope Pius XII defined the doctrine of the Assumption in these words: "We pronounce, declare, and define it to be a divinely revealed dogma that the Immaculate Mother of God, the ever Virgin Mary, having completed the course of her earthly life, was assumed body and soul into heavenly glory."[58] "Revealed dogma" here means "a fact contained within the deposit of revelation given to us by God, now solemnly proposed by the Pope to be believed as such by all the faithful."[59]

Mary is the first disciple, the pattern and type in faith and obedience of all the rest, Mother and first member of the Church. In her Assumption we see the pledge, the first fruits of our own glorious destiny. We celebrate, in the fact of her Assumption, her personal privilege and our promised glory. The mystery of the Assumption is a mystery of and for the whole Church. "In the most holy Virgin, the Church has already reached that perfection whereby she exists without spot or wrinkle" (Eph. 5:27).[60]

"We think that she, who has preceded the Church by her faith, she who preceded the Church in union with Christ, she who was there with Christ for the birth of the sacramental and hierarchical Church, preceded it also in its eternal destiny."[61] Many writers have noted the absence of historical record for the Assumption of Mary. Explicit historical and, indeed, liturgical testimony for the belief is lacking before the Syriac "*transitus*" fragment at the end of the fifth century and the Coptic liturgy, brought to the West by Cassian in the mid-sixth century.

There are also the imaginative tales called the "apocrypha." CRI says, "Since there was no authentic information [about the life and death of Mary], imagination ran wild creating legends."[62] "[T]here is nothing of any historical value in such apocryphal works."[63] "[The apocrypha] are filled with fantastic, absurd miracles, were written in poor taste, and contain bad theology. Yet historians recognize them to be the source from which the doctrine of Mary's assumption arose."[64]

Here I must blow the whistle. "Historians" who venture to engage in theology are straying from their field. Historians as such are not competent to make theological judgments. The Assumption is a theological datum and must be proved or disproved on theological, not historical grounds. The availability of historical evidence or the absence of it is strictly irrelevant to this discussion. Still more irrelevant, therefore, is the historical uselessness of the apocrypha. Pope Pius XII made no mention of the apocrypha in his definition of the Assumption. The doctrine and its definition do not rest on them.

The only interest of the apocrypha is that "they witness a popular belief among the faithful [of the fifth century] in the Assumption."[65] The apocrypha grew from this belief, not the belief from the apocrypha. The Anglican scholar Thomas Mozley writes, "The belief was never founded on that story. The story was founded on the belief. The belief, which was universal, required a definite shape, and that shape at length it found."[66]

J. Carol writes, "As historical accounts [the apocrypha] are valueless. But . . . they evidence the first unequivocal solutions to the problem of Mary's destiny. The solutions . . . disclose a genuinely Christian insight: It was not fitting that the body of Mary should see corruption. More importantly, the solution is given, incorruption is postulated, on theological lines: The principles of solution are the divine maternity, Mary's unimpaired virginity, her unrivaled holiness."[67]

CRI attacks: "The actual basis for the doctrine of the Assumption is a form of logic often employed in Catholic theology . . . God can do all things; it is proper that it should be so (e.g., that Mary should be assumed); therefore, God did it."[68] This is the "argument from fittingness," to which CRI objects, alleging that theologians who use it assume they know what is proper to God, whereas God's ways are not those of man (Is. 55:8–9).

The argument from fittingness has an honorable pedigree, which should be respected. The argument is implicit in the Bible itself. Look at Hebrews 2:10 and 7:26, for example. Furthermore, the argument is properly used, not as a substantive proof of a doctrine, but as a supportive suasion to a doctrine already proved. Fittingness was not invented by theologians. It comes to light by the working of the Holy Spirit in the Church, guiding it into the whole truth. "The Church [sees] the Assumption . . . implicitly contained within the complete notion of the divine maternity. 'The Church sees it there, not as the result of a logical deduction, still less as mere fittingness, but as one element of that miracle of miracles which God willed his Mother to be. The Church sees it with a supernatural insight imparted by the divine Spirit who dwells within her.'"[69]

"When the Church defines a truth, it does not canonize human logic. It defines because, under the guidance of the Spirit of truth, it discerns the truth. . . . It supposes a supernatural illumination proceeding from faith, grace, and the gifts of the Holy Spirit, a supernatural insight enabling the believer to discern, in fellowship with the Church, the implications of revelation proposed to him by the magisterium."[70] Catholics accept the teachings of the magisterium because we believe in Jesus Christ and in the promises he made to us about the work the Holy Spirit does in the Church: "The Advocate, the Holy Spirit that the Father will send in my name, he will teach you everything and remind you of all that I told you" John 14:26); "When he comes, the Spirit of truth, he will guide you to all truth" (John 16:13); "He who listens to you listens to me; he who rejects you rejects me" (Luke 10:16).

Without qualification, Jesus promised that the gates of hell would never prevail against his Church (Matt. 16:18), a promise that has failed if the Church has ever fallen or could fall into error in Christian doctrine. To think that Jesus could not, did not, or never intended to make good on these promises, that he left his Church to fall into any error whatever of doctrine or morality, is to question his power, his goodness, his truthfulness, and ultimately his divinity.

Paul teaches that the Church of the living God is the pillar and foundation of truth (1Tim. 3:15). He teaches that the relation of Christ to his Church is that of bridegroom to bride (Eph. 5:23–32). This teaching is true, and the Scripture cannot be broken: "The Church is subordinate to Christ" (v. 24)—not *was* or *may be* or *ought to have been*—but *is*. "Christ nourishes and cherishes the Church as his own flesh" (v. 29). Christ and the Church are one. Genesis 2:24, "the two of them become one flesh," used of man and wife in their marriage covenant, finds its ultimate meaning and fulfillment in the union between Christ and his Church. This "great mystery" (v. 32) is the marriage covenant between Christ and his Church.

Some accuse the Catholic Church of apostasy from Christ's teachings. It is his teachings that refute that charge. It is unbiblical to suggest that at some point in the third or fourth century (opponents are vague) Christ the bridegroom divorced his Church-bride on grounds of infidelity (from which he had *promised* to preserve her), lived a bachelor for about 1200 years, and then married more than 22,000 denominations.[71]

The Holy Spirit has been given to us and abides in us. God's gifts are irrevocable. "It is not that the word of God has failed . . . for the gifts and the call of God are irrevocable" (Rom. 9:6, 11:29). At this point, the infallibility of revelation meets the infallibility of the teaching Church, both guaranteed by the same Spirit: "The Holy Spirit, who revealed in the apostles, ever afterwards assists in the Church, that the Church may remember the truth in entirety, penetrate it deeply, and teach it alone."[72]

CRI moves on in its attack on the Assumption: "The [Catholic] church's first error was to regard its tradition as equal in authority to the Word of God. The second and potentially lethal error is to 'absolutize' the church's interpretation of both."[73] Here the article begs this question: Is the Word of God synonymous and coterminous with written Scripture? Is Scripture alone (*sola scriptura*) the Word of God and the repository of all his revelation? No, it is not. The revealed Word of God is contained in Scripture *and* oral Tradition.

Writing to the Thessalonians, Paul says: "He has also called you through *our gospel* to possess the glory of our Lord Jesus Christ. Therefore, brothers, stand firm and hold fast to the *traditions* that you were taught, either by an *oral statement* or by a *letter* of ours" (2 Thess. 2:14–15). Here the apostle equates his *gospel*, i.e., the Word of God that he has taught, with *traditions*. Then he distinguishes and divides these traditions into two: *oral statement* (oral Tradition) and *letter* (written Tradition), the latter of which in time would come to be recognized by the Church as sacred Scripture. CRI's error is to reject this Bible teaching, which witnesses to the equal dignity of oral and written Tradition.

Furthermore, in an important way, *oral* tradition holds the primacy. The earliest Christians until about A.D. 51 had none of the books of the New Testament, for none had yet been written. Of course, they had the Old Testament, but the whole message of Jesus and about Jesus was preserved as oral Tradition. The Church, then as now, regarded this Tradition as "equal in authority to the Word of God." Its Tradition about Jesus at that time was the New Covenant Word of God.

When New Testament Scripture was finally formed, it had to be *recognized as such* by the Church. This took considerable time. Nowhere in the written books of Scripture do we read the *titles* of the inspired books. Scripture does not provide its own canon—the Church did that, following its oral Tradition. Nowhere in any book of the Old or the New Testament is the principle *sola scriptura* (Scripture as the only source of revelation) to be found. This principle was invented centuries later and so falls under the stricture of Galatians 1:6–10. *It must be rejected if one wishes to follow the teachings of the Bible.*

CRI has rebuked the Church for "absolutizing" both Scripture and Tradition by defining doctrine, particularly the doctrine of Mary's Assumption. Now, fair is fair. If the Church in its earliest days absolutized its interpretations, which were the interpretations of its official teachers, the apostles, then it can and in fact it must do so today.

There is an distinction to be made here: The deposit of revelation was complete upon the death of the last apostle. The Church from that day proposes no new doctrine, but only works out the implications of the revelation entrusted to the apostles—and there *must be* implications for thinking people. The Church is thus the scribe instructed in the kingdom of heaven, like the head of a household who brings forth from his storeroom both the new and the old (Matt. 13:52).

From the very beginning, the Church, by its teaching authority, residing in the apostles and their successors, developed the implications of its doctrine and absolutized its oral Tradition. (Remember that at the beginning, from the first Pentecost, the Church had *only* oral Tradition about Jesus and his teaching.) Read the tenth, eleventh, and fifteenth chapters of Acts. In 10:9–16 Peter received a vision in which God revoked the Jewish kosher food laws. Shocked and doubtful, Peter pondered the vision. He became the type and figure of the Church's magisterium as it ponders the meaning of revelation. Peter then received a delegation of Gentiles, sent to beg him to come and visit the centurion Cornelius, a Gentile, in his home (vv. 17–23).

Why did he go with them, though it was "unlawful for a Jew to associate with or visit a Gentile" (v. 28)? He went because "God has shown me that I should not call any person profane or unclean" (v. 28). Peter engaged in the *development of doctrine*. His vision dealt with *animals*. By his apostolic authority Peter drew forth the vision's implication that no *person* is unclean. Later in Jerusalem, the Christians of the Judaizing faction confronted and rebuked Peter (11:2–3). He explained what had happened and so silenced them. As the events in Acts 10 and 11 were going on, everything was done orally. Writing it all down under divine inspiration, as Luke later did, did not increase its validity. Oral and written Tradition are equally valid, then as now. Acts 10 and 11 show that it is unbiblical to deny this.

Acts 15 is a mix of oral and written tradition, a point many non-Catholics miss: James quotes Old Testament Scripture (Amos 9:11–12), and the apostles and presbyters (the magisterium) write a letter, now a part of the New Testament, thanks to Luke and God's inspiration. There is plenty of discussion (oral Tradition), which Luke wove into his narrative, making it written Tradition or Scripture. CRI again misconstrues the facts and draws erroneous conclusions. Yet I agree with CRI on at least one point: What the Catholic Church does is lethal —not "lethal error," as CRI says, but lethal truth. The exercise of the Church's infallible mission slays the errors of *sola scriptura*, of private interpretation, and of general doctrinal muddleheadedness.

5

MARY'S SPIRITUAL MOTHERHOOD

✝

The Fathers of the Church, beginning with Justin (died A.D. 165) saw in Mary the antithesis of our natural mother, Eve. In Mary they contemplated the reversal of the drama of the first sin:

Eve listened to Satan under the guise of a serpent—Mary received the visitation of an angel.

Eve believed Satan's lie—Mary believed the truth of God's promise.

Eve disobeyed God's commandment—Mary obeyed God's word.

Eve is the mother of all the living, whom she and Adam involved in disaster; Mary is the Mother of all who live as co-heirs with Christ of eternal life, born from above through the death and resurrection of Jesus, the fruit of Mary's womb.

Mary's spiritual motherhood rests upon John 19:25–27: "Standing by the cross of Jesus were his mother and his mother's sister, Mary the wife of Clopas, and Mary

of Magdala. When Jesus saw his mother and the disciple
there whom he loved, he said to his mother, 'Woman, behold your son.' Then he said to the disciple, 'Behold your
mother.' And from that hour the disciple took her into his
home" (NAB). We believe that in the beloved disciple are
prefigured all the disciples of Christ. Thus, by his gift
from the cross, Christ makes Mary the spiritual mother of
us all. Jesus is her firstborn (Luke 2:7), the firstborn
among many brothers and sisters (Rom. 8:29). Mary is the
Mother of all those brothers and sisters, ourselves, destined for glory.

But CRI will have none of this. It begins the attack by
presenting Frank Sheed's explanation of Catholic doctrine:
"Calvary was the sacrifice of our race's redemption; everything that [Jesus] did and said on the cross related to that.
So with his word to our Lady and John. It was as part of
his plan of redemption that he was giving her to be the
mother of John—not of John as himself but as man. From
this moment she is the mother of us all."[74] CRI gives this
retort: "Protestants contend that only a predisposed am-
bition to produce a 'spiritual mother' could lead to such a
reading of the text. That Jesus had only John, and not all
men, in mind is made sufficiently clear by John's com-
ment that from that day on *he* took Mary into *his* care
[CRI's emphasis]. If the fact that Mary was now to look on
John as her son means that she was also to look on all believers as her children, then the fact that Mary was simul-
taneously entrusted to John's care would have to mean
that she was also entrusted to the care of all believers,

which is absurd."[75]

CRI is unqualified to pose as a champion for all—even most—Protestants. About Mary's motherhood of us all, the first Protestant Reformer, Martin Luther, said: "It is a great joy of which the angel speaks! It is God's consolation and overflowing goodness that man should be honored with such treasure: Mary as his true mother, Christ as his brother, and God as his Father."[76] On Christmas Day, 1523 Luther preached, "I believe that there is no one among us who would not leave his own mother to become a son of Mary. And that you can do, all the more because that has been offered as a choice to you, and it is an even greater joy than if you embraced your mother with real embraces."[77] Two days later he said, "We are the children of Mary; we are able to hear the song of the angels!"[78] At Christmas, 1529 Luther turned to the subject again: "Mary is the mother of Jesus and the mother of us all. If Christ is ours, we must be where he is, and where he is, we must be also, and all that he has must be ours, and his mother therefore also is ours."[79]

De Satgé writes, "She is the climax of the Old Testament people, the one to whom the cloud of witnesses from the ancient era look as their crowning glory, for it was through her response to grace that their Vindicator came to stand upon the earth. In the order of redemption she is the first fruits of her Son's saving work, the one among her Son's people who has gone all the way. And in the order of her Son's people, she is the mother."[80] Eastern Orthodox Christians, like Catholics, are firm in their allegiance to

Mary as Mother of us all. Nicolas Zernov writes, "The
Mother of God is the Mother of all mankind, the friend
and protectress of all members of the Church."[81] On this
doctrine of Mary's universal motherhood, Orthodox and
Catholic Christians are unanimous; Protestants are a house
not just separated but divided. Many Protestants agree
with the liturgical churches; some do not, but CRI suggests *all* do not. This is simply inaccurate. If CRI is sincere in its concern for ecumenism, it will cease attacking
the Catholic Church's understanding of our (common)
Mother. It will make every effort to unite Protestants in a
devotion to Mary at least as warm as Luther's.

CRI characterizes Frank Sheed's Catholic interpretation of John 19:25–27 as "absurd." It objects that if Mary
must look on all of us as her children, then she would have
to be entrusted to the care of all believers, as she was entrusted to John's care. This objection collapses when we
look to the Greek text of John 19:27: "the disciple took
her *eis ta idia*." CRI follows the Anchor Bible translation
of the three Greek words, translating them as "into his
care." Other translations, Catholic and non-Catholic, have
"into his home" (NAB, NIV, NEB, CCD, Kleist-Lilly) or
"to his own home" (RSV) or *"chez lui"* (Jerusalem) or *"en
su casa"* (BAC).

Such translations do very well for spiritual reading, but
they are too free for exegesis. They are, in fact, precise
where the Greek is vague. In the phrase *eis ta idia*, there is
no word meaning "care" or "house" or "home." (One may
refer by contrast to John 7:53: "They went each to his own

house" (RSV), where John wrote *oikon* [house] in his Greek text.) What does *eis ta idia* mean, then?

Eis is a preposition with five general meanings, expressing place, time, measure, relationship, and end, purpose, or goal. (The last two meanings—relationship and end, purpose, or goal—frequently converge in a given sentence.) *Ta idia* is the neuter plural substantive use of the adjective *idios*: "private, one's own." John has used the plural, although the singular *to idion* is often found with no difference of meaning. According to context, the meaning may be "one's own, my own, your own, his own, her own, our own, their own."

But one's own *what*? There is the rub. John's expression is neuter and therefore, one may say, deliberately noncommittal. *Ta idia* can mean one's own things, purposes, opinions, property, interests, intentions, business, whatever.

Consider classical writers. Euripides (*Iphigenia in Aulis*, 1363) writes *idia prasson,* "doing his own thing." (Paul [1 Thess. 4:11] uses almost the same words: *prassein ta idia,* "to do your own business.") Again, Euripides (*Phoenician Maidens*, 555) writes, "Mortals do not possess things as their own [*idia*]," and (*Andromache,* 376) he says, "True friends have nothing as their own [*idion*]." Xenophon (*Anabasis* 1, 3, 3) writes of "[money] which I did not put away for my own [personal use, *eis to idion*]"—like John's *eis ta idia*, except that John uses the plural. Similar uses of the substantive *idion/idia* are found in Antiphon, Andocides, Isocrates, Demosthenes, Lucian, Theognis, and other

Greek writers of the classical and post-classical periods.

Eis in John 19:27 is used to express end, purpose, or goal, a frequent usage in John's Gospel (1:7, 4:14, 4:36, 6:9, 9:39, 12:7, 13:29, 18:37). In this usage *eis* translates into English as "for" or "as." That the disciple took Mary *eis ta idia* means only that he took her *as his own*.

We teach and believe that John here is a type of all disciples. We all take Christ's Mother by his gift *as our own*. She is the Mother of us all. This understanding is explained by John Paul II, quoting Augustine: "Clearly, in the Greek text, the expression *eis ta idia* goes beyond the mere acceptance of Mary by the disciple in the sense of material lodging and hospitality in his house; it indicates rather a communion of life established between the two as a result of the words of the dying Christ; cf. Saint Augustine, *In Joan. Evang. Tract.* 119, 3: CCL 36, 659: 'He took her to himself, not into his own property, for he possessed nothing of his own, but among his own duties, which he attended to with dedication.'"[82] In John 1:11-14, the apostle uses the phrase *eis ta idia* with *eis* in its local meaning of *to* or *into*: "He came to his own" (neuter). This is followed at once by the masculine *hoi idioi*—"his own people" (who refused to accept him.) On his cross the order is reversed. He comes to *hoi idioi,* his own people, his beloved disciple and his mother, and they willingly accept him, and they do his will. Obedient to his command, they take each other as their own (*ta idia*). The disciple takes Mary as his Mother, and she takes him as her son. The two of them on Calvary are types of the Church, paradigms of all Christ's disciples. She is our Mother. We are her sons and daughters. Paul calls Jesus "the firstborn among many brothers and sisters" (Rom. 8:29). Shared humanity and grace makes him our brother, and the Mother of our brother by nature and grace is our Mother too.

CRI alleges, "Our life *is* contained in the life of the Son, and Mary *is* His mother [CRI's emphasis]. But this does not make her our mother in any way. . . . The birth that Jesus had through [sic] Mary was according to the flesh. Jesus derived His physical life through [sic] Mary, but that is not what He came to communicate to us."[83] But it is precisely by the human nature which he took from Mary that "the Word became flesh and dwelt among us" (John 1:14). Because of her free cooperation, he has that body in which God became visible to us, and we could see his glory, full of grace and truth. From her he received the Body and Blood which are our Eucharistic food and drink, the pledge and guarantee of our eternal life (John 6:33ff, 50, 53, 57). Jesus does not communicate himself to us in any other way than by what he is, God and man now inseparably united in one divine Person, Son of God and Mary's son. In and by *both* his natures, human and divine, the one Person Jesus is our Savior, and his human nature is from Mary.

Now, let us ask a further question: Were Mary's birth-giving and motherhood purely physical? Among human beings, motherhood is higher than among other animals because it is a relation of one *person*, the mother, to another *person*, the child. Since human persons are free and intelligent beings animated by spiritual, immortal souls, there is a spiritual component in all human motherhood. But Mary's motherhood is unique in that her child is a divine Person. The union of divine nature and human nature in Mary's womb was supernatural in origin—"the Holy Spirit will come upon you, and the power of the Most High will overshadow you" (Luke 1:35).

Her preparation, too, for motherhood was supernatural, not merely physical. God had filled her utterly with his presence and his grace before the angel approached her (1:28). Her personal response to the angel's message was prompted by the God-given grace moving within her. That response was flawless. She was humble (1:48), full of faith (1:45), and obedient to God's call (1:38). These Bible truths about Mary led Augustine to exclaim that she conceived Christ in her mind and heart before she conceived him in her womb. Mary can be spiritually our Mother and spiritually the Mother of the beloved disciple because she was spiritually—not merely physically—the Mother of Christ.

CRI denies that there is a *biblical* basis for saying that everything Jesus said on the cross has a redemptive significance. I repeat: Jesus' words on the cross to Mary and the disciple, says CRI, have *no redemptive significance*; therefore, they do not apply to *all the redeemed*. CRI here falters as a Bible-Christian organization, and many Protestants will have yet another reason for rejecting its article as a "Protestant response" speaking for all Protestants.

Second Timothy 3:15–16 says, "The sacred Scriptures are capable of giving you wisdom for *salvation through faith in Christ Jesus. All* [repeat, *all*] Scripture is inspired by God and is useful . . . for training in *righteousness*."

We know that the writers of all four Gospels were selective in their choice of the materials available to them from oral tradition. John tells us clearly what his own principle of selection was. "Now Jesus did many other signs in the presence of [his] disciples that are not written in this book. But *these* are written that you may come to *believe* that Jesus is the Messiah, the Son of God, and that *through this belief you may have life in his name*" (John 20:30–31). What this means is that every detail of John's Gospel has redemptive significance. The *biblical* basis for that should be abundantly clear—but apparently it is not, at least to CRI.

We must notice the position of the words in John 19:28: "After this, aware that everything was now finished. . . ." What was finished? His redemptive sacrifice, for Jesus' death follows immediately, with his taking the sip of common wine (19:29) and with his last words, "It is finished." But *when* was he aware that everything was now finished? Precisely when he had made provision for his Church in 19:27, by giving us his own Mother. Verses 18–24 portray the crucifixion with its attendant circumstances. Verse 30 records his death. Between these two events of utmost redemptive significance are verses 25-27. What happens in them? A private little family arrangement? No, a redemptive act: the bestowal of his own

Mother to be Mother of the household of God, his Church, and Mother of every disciple-member of his Church.

6

COREDEMPTRIX
AND MEDIATRIX

✝

CRI next turns its guns on the titles "coredemptrix" and "mediatrix," with which Catholics sometimes invoke Mary. "Coredemptrix" implies that Mary cooperated with her Son in redeeming mankind; "mediatrix" means that, in subordination to Christ, she promotes our access to the Father. (As CRI notes, "mediatrix" may include also the title "dispensatrix," which implies that Mary has a role to play in the distribution of graces of redemption to us, her children.) CRI quotes Catholic theologian Ludwig Ott: "'Behold the handmaid of the Lord; be it done to me according to thy word.' The Incarnation of the Son of God and the redemption of mankind by the vicarious atonement of Christ were dependent on her assent."[84] CRI writes, "Nowhere does the Bible teach such an inflated conception of Mary's role—as though the fate of all humanity was hanging on her choice. God determined before time began that he would redeem the world through the death of his Son. . . . No human being could have stood in the way of this; to hold otherwise would mean denying the *central* biblical doctrine of God's sovereignty" (CRI's emphasis).[85]

I fear that CRI has made up its mind and does not wish to be bothered by the facts—in this case, by the fact that Catholics, whose belief is as Ott describes it, nevertheless affirm God's supreme sovereignty. Another fact which CRI ignores is human freedom, a biblical doctrine as well as a fact of our daily experience. Reconciling God's supreme dominion with human freedom, while doing violence to neither, is one of theology's knottiest problems—certainly not one to be solved in this article. Yet the Bible does teach that we are free and that we *can* throw a wrench into the engine of God's eternal plans—in fact, we often have. Man cannot ultimately defeat God's purposes, but by God's permission and providence man can certainly sabotage them temporarily.

In the Old Testament, God made covenant after covenant with his people, and time after time his people (or certain key individuals among them) upset God's plans by abusing their freedom. They sinned. Think of Adam and Eve (Gen. 3), Cain (Gen. 4), Noah and his brood (Gen. 9:18–27), the sons of Samuel (1Sam. 8:1–22), Saul (1 Sam. 15:10–31; 28:15–19). Think of the denunciations of Isaiah (65:12) and Jeremiah (7:13–15). Think, above all, of the terrible recriminations of Jesus in Matthew 21:33–45 and 23:29–38. His words are clear: "I yearned to gather your children together. . . . but *you* were unwilling!"

Of course, Mary was free to say "no" to God's invitation. She was free because she was human, and her value to God, who wanted to become human, was that his prospective Mother was *fully* human. If he had forced her, or if he had subtracted her freedom from her humanity, she would have been left an un-person, subhuman. Does any Bible Christian really suppose that Jesus was mothered by a zombie? That would surely be unbiblical; it would even be un-Protestant.

Martin Luther said, "The holy Virgin would never have conceived the Son of God if she had not believed the annunciation of the angel."[86] But belief is a free human act, assisted by God's grace. John Calvin wrote in his *Commentary on Luke* (1:42, 45), "Now she is called blessed; receiving by faith the blessing which is offered to her, *she opened the way for God to accomplish his work*" (emphasis mine). The Anglican de Satgé writes, "She was chosen, but the dialogue in Luke's account shows that her own response was not a foregone conclusion. She asked for clarifications and she was given them. . . . . Mary exercised her free choice to accept God's choice of her."[87]

Evangeline Cory Booth, the daughter of General William Booth, founder of the Salvation Army, was no theologian, but she was a good Protestant and a fair thinker. In a lecture, she said, "The free agency of man is a cardinal truth accepted by the whole Church. We are all free to accept or reject God's plan for us. *The whole Bible proves this* [emphasis mine]. Mary is no exception to the rule. Mary might have refused. . . . The angel Gabriel was sent, not only to make the annunciation, but to gain Mary's concurrence or consent to fall in with God's will."[88]

CRI refers to Psalm 115:3 to "prove" Mary had no freedom to refuse her calling: "Our God is in heaven; whatever he wills, he does." It is dangerous to read a Bible verse in isolation. First Timothy 2:4 says, "God . . . wills everyone to be saved and to come to knowledge of the truth," but Matthew 25:41 opens up the possibility that some will *not* be saved.

Is God's dominion threatened by sinners' free refusal of his saving grace? Obviously not. The world's salvation certainly was determined in God's eternal decree, but Mary's freedom was budgeted for in that same eternal decree. If Mary had backed down, God would have found some other way to accomplish his designs. But since she did freely assent, Mary participates in our redemption at its very source. Therefore, in an entirely subordinate, creaturely way, empowered entirely by God's redeeming grace, she is a "coredeemer." "If our attitude towards divine plans is not docile, not even God can act. But in faith Mary consented, and consenting she believed. Nothing could henceforth arrest the efficacy of the divine advances; in Mary, humanity had made an act of saving faith."[89]

CRI denies that Mary is in any sense associated with Christ in the distribution of his graces to us, objecting that the eternal Logos (Christ) was not Mary's to give: "Mary was merely the vehicle the Triune God chose for the Logos's entry into this world."[90] (Yes, Virginia, CRI actually calls Mary a "vehicle"!) "In Scripture," CRI continues, "after this miracle is accomplished, she recedes into the background, and we read little about her."[91] Little, perhaps, but that little is much: Everywhere that Mary appears, she is important; she steadily counterpoints her Son. In her last appearance on earth (Acts 1:14) she is at prayer with the brothers and sisters of her firstborn (Rom. 8:29), who are, in a spiritual sense, her children too, as they wait with her for the coming of the Holy Spirit. Who will dare to say that her prayers and theirs had nothing to do with the Spirit's coming?

The core of CRI's rejection of Mary's subordinate mediation is its interpretation of 1 Timothy 2:5, "For there is one God. There is also one mediator between God and the human race, Christ Jesus, himself human, who gave himself as ransom for all." I might add the words of Peter in Acts 4:12: "There is salvation in no one else, for there is no other name under heaven by which we must be saved."

CRI lists several texts from Hebrews (2:16–18, 4:14–16; 7:23–28; 8:1, 6, 13; 9:12–14, 24–26; 10:1–22) which illustrate this "major theme of the New Testament."[92] To say Mary is coredeemer and mediatrix, alleges CRI, is to violate this Bible teaching. But why does Paul's affirmation of Jesus as the one mediator come where it does in 1 Timothy? In 2:1–2 he recommends that Timothy's church members pray for *all* men (even rulers—in that time of persecution of Christians by the Roman authorities!) In 2:3–4 he reassures Timothy that such prayer is good and pleasing to God our Savior. Why? Because

God "wills *everyone* to be saved." In the key text, 2:5, Paul gives the *reason* for his insistence upon prayer for *pagans*: "For there is *one* God . . . *one* mediator between God and the human race, Christ Jesus . . . who gave himself as ransom for *all*."

The principal point of Paul's teaching in 2:1–5 is that we must pray for everybody because God is everybody's God. There is no other. Christ alone is for *everyone* the only way to the Father. Gentiles, even harsh rulers, are men and women. Christ the God-Man is their Christ too. He is the go-between for them and not just for us. Paul hammers this teaching home in 2:6–7 by noting that Christ gave himself as a ransom for *all*, not just for those already Christian. Paul reminds Timothy and his group that he (Paul) was appointed preacher and apostle to the Gentiles (*Gentiles* yet!). The fact is that in 1 Timothy 2:1–7 (the whole context, mind you), Paul commands *all* Christians to be mediators and intercessors for all men because God is God of all and Christ is Christ for all. He concludes by saying that he himself is a mediator too, as preacher and apostle.

The high point of the passage is verse 5, where he enthrones Christ, the mediator par excellence, who by uniting us to himself makes mediators of us all for all. The whole passage, verses 1–7, is a unit and must be read as a unit. Its message is broadly ecumenical; it is a missionary message, a message of outreach. By a sad irony, CRI misreads the message, shatters it, and uses one shard (verse 5 out of context) as a shibboleth for a narrow brand of "reformist" theology. Contradicting its own position, CRI oddly concludes, "Believers *are* called to participate subordinately in Christ's mediating work (e.g., 1 Pet. 2:9, 2 Cor. 5:20). . . . As mediators, believers can represent God to man (through proclaiming his word) and man to God (through prayer)."[93] At this admission I am ready to quit the field of battle, rejoicing in victory. But CRI illogically goes on: "This is not the issue!" (Isn't it?) The issue, it seems, is this: "While others beside Christ can play mediating roles between man and God, there is a line of demarcation that *separates* [my emphasis and shock] the mediation of Christ from that of all others; certain critical attributes and functions that *only* he can possess and perform." And here is the nub of the objection: "[I]n certain significant respects, Catholicism places Mary on Christ's side of the line."[94]

Not only is Christ like us in everything, sin alone excepted (Heb. 4:15), but he has joined his members to himself in a union of life and love, in which we are living branches of Christ the vine (John 15:5), members of his body the Church (1 Cor. 12:13, 27). It is this union with Christ which empowers us to produce the fruit of good works. This is faith working through love and not any power originating in us. We share the nature of God (2 Pet. 1:4) through our identity as the Church (Acts 9:4–5).

We also share his priesthood. CRI blows smoke by talking about Mary's diminishing the "all-sufficiency and glory of Christ's priesthood," the "uniqueness of his priestly role," the "integrity of his high priesthood."[95]

Nonsense. It is Christ himself who has given all his members, Mary included, a share in his own priesthood. "He has made us into a kingdom, priests for his God and Father" (Rev. 1:6, 5:10, 20:6). We share in his priesthood, our Mother and ourselves, all his disciples (1 Pet. 2:5, 9).

But what about the priestly function of making expiation for sin? *Every* Christian including Mary must do this in Christ—that is what taking up our cross daily and following him means. "Christ's sufferings overflow to us" (2 Cor. 1:5). "I rejoice in my sufferings for your sake, and in my flesh I am filling up what is lacking in the afflictions of Christ, on behalf of his body, the Church" (Col. 1:24). That is shared priestly expiation. We are partners and co-operators with Christ in our own salvation and in the redemption of others. We are *all*, in a sense, coredeemers and mediators with him, Mother and children alike. How? Why? Because that is the way his love has arranged our salvation. The branches live with the life of the vine, and the *branches* bear the fruit of eternal life (John 15:5-8), because they are united to Christ the vine.

Now, about praying to Mary, the saints, and the angels: This is a complete no-no, says CRI. "No departed believer is shown in Scripture to be the object of prayer. Biblically, when a man (or woman) prays, he talks to God through the mediation of the God-man, Jesus Christ. No heavenly entities other than the persons of the Trinity figure into the picture."[96]

Untrue. Jesus the mediator is the head of a host of subordinate mediators—his members, his branches—who, because of their oneness with him, share in his priestly activity, part of which is intercession.

The vine and the body are metaphors for the Church. The Church is not a collection of isolated individuals, but a family of adopted brothers and sisters of Christ, children of God (2 Cor. 6:18). We are members of one another (Eph. 4:25), and it is God's will for us to have concern for one another (1 Cor. 12:25). We are the household of God (1 Tim. 3:15), both here and forever in heaven (Rev. 13:6). Our members in heaven are not "dispensed" from having concern for us still on earth. That they are aware of us and concerned for us is the teaching of Hebrews 12:1–2. "Since we are surrounded by so great a cloud of witnesses [the saints in heaven, Heb. 11], let us rid ourselves of every burden and sin . . . and persevere . . . while keeping our eyes fixed on Jesus." This text means that these heavenly witnesses are a help to us in our efforts, and their help is integrated and finds its goal in Jesus.

In Revelation 4:4, 10; 5:8, twenty-four "elders" engage in worship before the throne of God and of the Lamb. Are these elders saints in heaven, or are they angels? It would seem they are human, because they are distinguished from angels in 5:11. Whoever they are, these heavenly worshipers are involved with us and our concerns, because each of them holds a golden bowl "filled with incense which is the prayers of the holy ones" (5:8). The "holy ones" or "saints" are, in New Testament language, the members of the Church on earth (Rev. 13:7). So the heavenly elders offer our prayers to God as part of their own divine worship.

None of this biblical witness has any meaning to one who denies that we on earth can pray to our Mother and to our siblings in heaven, the saints. To be in heaven is to love to perfection (1 Cor. 13:8, 13). Do the saints in heaven love God? Do they love their brothers and sisters still on earth? If they do, then how do they express and manifest this love for us? By praying for us, of course. They have no other way.

Can we, on our part, from down here, get in touch with them, pray to them, ask their prayers? Christians have always done so, with God's full approval. Our God is the Father of an adopted family. He loves us. He is not a dog-in-the-manger God. He is not insecure, threatened when his children show love for and trust in one another. He is not paranoid nor miserly of his own glory. He welcomes our prayers to his angels and saints, and he welcomes their intercession on our behalf. There is nothing in the Bible which contradicts Catholic belief and practice here and much in the Bible which teaches and supports the Catholic doctrine of the communion of saints.[97]

CRI objects that Catholics "link Mary in the heavenly chain between Jesus and man" and so "place Mary in a mediating position unoccupied by other believers." This supposedly "depreciates the all-sufficiency and glory of Christ's priesthood."[98] Mary certainly has a special place among us because she is both Mother and first disciple of our Redeemer. She is more exalted and her prayers are more powerful because she is holier than all the other saints and all the angels; after all, "The fervent prayer of a righteous person is very powerful" (Jas. 5:16). CRI then makes a damaging admission: "While some [disciples] may be more *effective* in prayer because of the moral character of their lives (Jas. 5:16b), they all stand on the same *ground*, which has nothing to do with their personal holiness."[99] CRI admits, therefore, that Mary's prayers are effective since she is holy, "full of grace" (Luke 1:28). But what does it *mean* that all disciples (Mary included) stand on the same *ground*?

CRI explains: "The Church portrays the *basis* for Mary's mediation as being more like that of Christ than that of other believers. Christ is qualified to serve as mediator between man and God because of his absolute holiness (Heb. 7:26). Believers, on the other hand, all are qualified to pray—for themselves or others—*strictly* on the basis of Christ's imputed merits, received through faith (Rom. 3:21–28; Eph. 3:12). . . . But Mary serves as mediatrix on the basis of her perfect holiness—the same basis Christ serves on. . . . Even if we grant that this holiness is the 'imparted righteousness of Christ,' *as the church teaches* [emphasis mine], it is still in a real sense *hers*. This places her in a similar light as Christ, again diluting the uniqueness of his priestly role."[100]

CRI has blundered badly by confusing the *essence* of Christ's mediation with the personal holiness which *befits* him as mediator. The *ground* upon which Christ *alone* can stand, and by virtue of which he exercises mediation, is not his holiness, but his *Incarnation*, the hypostatic union of the human nature and the divine in the one divine Person of the Word.

Not only is CRI confused in this part of its article, but its claim contradicts another statement in the same article, which, in fact, got the matter right: "This is the significance of the Incarnation: Because he is man, *Christ is able to function as our mediator* [emphasis mine]; because he is God, we have *direct* access into the presence of deity and never have to settle for anything less."[101]

Of course, Mary does *not* stand upon the same "ground" as Christ. He alone is the Word made flesh. But on two accounts she is superior to us: in discipleship and in holiness, holiness being closeness of union with Christ and, through him, with the Father and the Holy Spirit. She directly ministered to the second Person of the Blessed Trinity, when he took flesh from her in her womb, assuming human nature in the hypostatic union. (In simple terms, Mary is the Mother of God because her child is God.) Secondly, she has received more grace from him than we and has used it far better than we, being sinless from her creation and through all of her pilgrimage on earth. Her fullness of grace means far more than her utter freedom from sin. It includes all God's gifts to her, especially her vocation as Mother of God.

I shall now try to abbreviate the next part of CRI's attack on our Church and our Mother in a series of statements based—I hope not too loosely—on the text of the article.[102]

*1. If Mary can influence her Son to help us, he must oth-
erwise be less disposed to do so.*

I answer this objection with Mary's words in John
2:1–11: "They have no wine!" "Woman, what's that to
you and me? My hour has not yet come." "Do whatever he
tells you." "Draw out now and take the wine to the head-
waiter." I would not say Christ showed himself "less disposed" to help the newlyweds here. He simply and freely
had given his Mother a role to play in the bestowal of his
gift. He still does—all the time, in all his dealings with
us.

*2. Catholics claim that apart from Mary's mediation,
Christ himself would not be perfectly reconciled to us.*

I answer that, from the beginning, God in his work of
perfect reconciliation included Mary as Christ's minister,
associate, and disciple in her own salvation and in ours.
First, she is a believer, a Christian: "Blessed are you who
believe" (Luke 1:45). Second, since Mary is a believer, she
is in Christ (John 15:1–5, 17:22–23, Rom. 12:4–5, 1 Cor.
10:16, 12:12–27). Third, because Mary is in Christ her
prayers are efficacious and powerful (Jas. 5:16).

*3. Either Mary's role is superfluous or Christ's mediation
is inadequate.*

I answer that Christ mediates between humans (including Mary) and the Father by uniting us to himself in a vital union of members to head, branches to vine. Since he has assumed our human nature from her alone, her role in his plan is unique. Yet it is all his plan. No one, Mary included, has anything except from him. But as we are members of one another, we enjoy one another and we pray for one another. God wills this. We are not "superfluous" for one another. (With this in mind, I often now pray for the people at the *Christian Research Journal*, and I invite the reader to join me.)

CRI then sketchily notices the problem of justification and salvation, a matter about which Catholics and Protestants tend to disagree. "In the Protestant view, salvation is *assured* [my emphasis] to the true believer, because it has been *received* as a *gift* by *grace* through *faith* (Eph. 2:8–9; Rom. 3:21–24). Thus, since *the Christian is already saved*, etc."[103] This doctrine of the absolute assurance of salvation hews closely to the Reformation line and so strays far from the Bible.

The Bible teaches that faith in Jesus Christ is *necessary* for salvation. It nowhere says that faith is *sufficient* for salvation, and it nowhere says that an individual possesses *certainty* of his own salvation. Paul was certainly a Christian who believed in "salvation through faith in Christ Jesus" (2 Tim. 3:15), but he was not self-complacent, so as to say, "I know for a fact I am going to heaven." He says of himself, "I am not aware of anything against myself, but I am not thereby acquitted. It is the Lord who judges me. *Therefore do not pronounce judgment before the time, before the Lord comes*" (1 Cor. 4:4–5). Again, he says, "I do not run aimlessly, I do not box as one beating the air; but I chastise my body and bring it under subjection, lest after preaching to others I myself should be disqualified" (1 Cor. 9:27; see also Rom. 11:22, 2 Cor. 11:31).

The Bible teaches that effort in good works and penance are necessary for salvation, as Christ taught (Luke 9:23, 13:3–5, 14:27).[104] Paul says we hold the treasure of God's grace in earthen vessels (2 Cor. 4:7). This alone should keep us from self-complacency in our faith. "Let anyone who thinks that he stands take heed lest he fall" (1 Cor. 10:12). He teaches the need for personal examination of conscience, especially before receiving Christ in the Eucharist (1 Cor. 11:28), and he makes this powerful plea against self-complacency: "Work out your salvation with fear and trembling" (Phil. 2:12).

Peter teaches us the need for sobriety and watchfulness against temptation, and he warns us we have to win our salvation in suffering with Christ (1 Pet. 5:8-10). James is clearest of all in teaching that faith is not sufficient for salvation: "Even the demons believe—and tremble" (Jas. 2:19). His teaching accords with Paul's: If we are to be saved, good living is required, patience and perseverance in good works (Rom. 2:7, Gal. 6:7–10, 2 Thess. 3:12–13).

We should have faith in Jesus, not faith in faith. Faith is a daily recommitment to him, not a once-for-all thing. It lives and grows as we do. It is Christ-centered, leaving ourselves and our destiny in his hands because we are sure he loves us. Egotism cannot live with authentic Bible-faith, but it easily creeps in to a once-for-all, complacent faith. We should reflect that this once-for-all faith was absolutely unknown before Martin Luther, who even wanted to take the epistle of James out of the Bible because James teaches so clearly that faith alone is not sufficient. This Luther-faith is not Bible-faith and should be rejected because it is "another gospel" (Gal. 1:8–9).

CRI also does not like us to say that Mary is the Mother of mercy. Nor does it wish us to think that, because of Mary's intercession, we have nothing to fear from Jesus, our judge. We are told that this flies in the face of Hebrews 4:15–16 (it doesn't, as a matter of fact). First John 5:16 tells us to pray for the sinner, and God will give him life.

If, because of Tom's, Dick's, and Harry's intercession, God will give the sinner life so that he has nothing to fear from Jesus the judge, I should think that Mary also qualifies to intercede with her Son. Since Mary is the Mother of the whole Church, indeed of all mankind, her intercession extends to us all. This is the way God has arranged matters with us. Mary's intercession with her Son, claims CRI, "makes hollow the Church's assurance that Mary's mediation 'neither takes away anything from nor adds anything to the dignity and efficacy of Christ the one mediator.'"[105] I say, if the Church's assurance seems hollow to the folks at the Christian Research Institute, I regret their reluctance to believe, but Catholics must and will continue to follow the gospel anyway.

7

QUEEN
OF HEAVEN

✝

A beautiful hymn, found in many Protestant hymnals, shows that Protestants are comfortable calling God and Christ "King." It begins, "Come, worship the King, all glorious above!" Although Protestants call Christ the King, it is not usual among them to call the King's Mother their Queen.

Catholics believe she is indeed our Queen and that her spiritual royalty flows from and is subordinate to Christ's kingship. The ground of Mary's queenship is her role in our redemption. Pope Pius XII taught that "Jesus Christ alone, God and man, is King in the full, proper, and absolute sense of the term. Mary also, in a restricted and only analogous way, shares in his royal dignity as the Mother of Christ who is God, as his associate in the work of Redemption, in his conflict with the enemy, and in his complete victory. From this association with Christ the King, she obtains a height of splendor unequaled in all creation."[106] In God's plan, Mary consented to give birth to the Savior *precisely as Savior and King* (Matt. 1:21, Luke 1:32–33). Her words, "Be it done to me according to your word," were her pledge to live for her Son to the end, through contradiction and through the sword of sorrow which would pierce her heart as she stood beneath his cross.

Her queenship, like her Son's kingdom (John 18:36), is not of this world. Her role is to draw people to acknowledge and follow Jesus as their Lord and King. The Bible prefigures her role in her instruction to the waiters at the marriage feast in Cana (John 2:5); in her acceptance of the beloved disciple as her son, a type of all Christ's disciples in every age (John 19:26); and in her presence and prayer as a member of the tiny Church in the upper room, where the first Christians waited for the Holy Spirit to enliven them all (Acts 1:14, 2:1–41). Mary's queenship is spiritual and ecclesial leadership, not exercised as a member of the hierarchy, which she was not, but by holy example and all-embracing intercession.

Catholics share this belief in Mary's queenship with Christians of the Eastern rites, both Catholic and non-Catholic. Eastern Christians, whose main turf stretches from Poland to Sakhalin and from the Sudan to the White Sea, pray in these words: "I will open my mouth, and it shall be filled with the Spirit; I will break forth into a hymn to the Queen Mother. . . . I will sing her privileges with exultation" (*The Akathistos Hymn*).

For Eastern Christians, Mary is "Queen of creation," "Queen who saves by intercession," "glorious Lady, Queen who stands at the Lord's right hand." In Egypt and Ethiopia Christians hail "the Virgin, the very and true Queen, glory of our race." She is the "Queen of love." The Western Syrian rite, centered upon Antioch, prays, "Lord, you have made her Queen of the heavenly spirits and of those who dwell on earth. . . . Grant to us to feel at every moment the effect of the prayers which she makes for us; and *help her that she will favor us*, so that we will be protected" (emphasis mine—notice how clearly Mary's *subordination* to Christ in her queenship is expressed). At the Incense Prayer, Mary is called "Immaculate Virgin, Mother, Queen of Angels and Empress of Saints." (In far-off Germany, hundreds of years after this Syrian prayer was composed, Martin Luther would call Mary "more than an Empress," as we shall later see.)

The Eastern Syrian or Chaldean rite in Iraq, Iran, and Malabar celebrates Mary as "Mother of the King of kings." The Christians of this rite pray, "O Queen of queens, all rich, enrich with benefits your servants, O Mother of the Most High! For he has made you the dispenser of his treasures and universal Queen, for it has pleased the King of kings to place you over all. By your goodness, pour out on all the gifts they need, so that the whole world may prepare for you a crown of thanks."

To Armenian Christians, Mary is "Queen of the world," "Queen of the universe, who carried in her arms him before whom the celestial spirits tremble." "We, the human race, we glorify thee, Mother of God, whom the angelic powers honor."[107] Christians who do not acknowledge

Mary as their Queen are thus out of step with the vast majority of their fellow Christians, both Catholic and non-Catholic. A true concern for ecumenism would lead them to *join* us in devotion to Mary—or at least to refrain from attacking her. The subtitle of the entire CRI article is: "From Lowly Handmaid to Queen of Heaven." We are supposed to see an anomaly here: "How could a mere village girl, a lowly handmaid, *ever* become Queen of heaven?" The answer to this objection is in our Lord's words of reproach to the Sadducees about another matter: "Are you not misled, because you do not know the scriptures or the power of God?" (Mark 12:24).

Scripture is full of the promise that the lowly and poor will be raised to royal dignity: "From the ash-heap he lifts up the poor . . . to make a glorious throne their heritage" (1 Sam. 2:8); "You who have followed me will yourselves sit on twelve thrones, judging the twelve tribes of Israel" (Matt. 19:28); "If we persevere, we shall also reign with him" (2 Tim. 2:12); "I will give the victor the right to sit with me on my throne, as I myself first won the victory and sit with my Father on his throne" (Rev. 3:21). It would be unbiblical to deny this victory and share in Jesus' royal Davidic throne to his Mother.

Jesus again said to his apostles, "It is you who have stood by me in my trials, and I confer a kingdom on you, just as my Father has conferred one on me" (Luke 22:28–29). But who stood by him most faithfully? The apostles fled at Jesus' arrest. Only one, the beloved disciple, dared to stand beneath the cross. But Mary stood by him there, and so he will confer the kingdom on her.

Christopher O'Donnell points out the remarkable parallel between Luke 1 and Philippians 2:5–11, between Jesus and Mary as examples of poverty and humility raised to unimaginable glory:

"It is worth remarking that the great hymn of redemption in Philippians 2:5–11 finds echoes in the first chapter of St. Luke's Gospel. Jesus took the form of a slave (Greek *doulos,* Phil. 2:7); Mary describes herself as a slave (Greek *doule,* Luke 1:38). Jesus humbled himself (Phil. 2:8); Mary describes her state as one of humiliation (Luke 1:48). God exalted Jesus (Phil. 2:9); the humble are exalted (Luke 1:52). Every knee shall bend . . .. confess that Jesus is Lord (Phil. 2:11); all generations will call Mary blessed (Luke 1:48). The similarity of Greek expressions throughout seems to suggest deliberate borrowing by Luke to illustrate the mystery of poverty being exalted in both Son and mother. . . . One can at least point to a common tradition to which Paul and Luke had access."[108]

Every disciple will share Jesus' royal dignity. But Mary is the first and holiest disciple, "full of grace" and first to believe in him (Luke 1:28,45). She is even—unimaginable dignity!—the very Mother of her Lord (1:43). This translates to Queen, if human language and divine revelation have any meaning at all. Although Martin Luther was somewhat nervous about applying the title "Queen of Heaven" to Mary, he admits that "it is a true enough name and yet does not make her a goddess."[109]

In a sermon Luther preached on July 2, 1532, the Feast

of the Visitation, he said, "She, the Lady above heaven and earth, must . . . have a heart so humble that she might have no shame in washing the swaddling clothes or preparing a bath for St. John the Baptist, like a servant girl. What humility! It would surely have been more just to have arranged for her a golden coach, pulled by 4,000 horses, and to cry and proclaim as the carriage proceeded: 'Here passes the woman who is raised far above all women, indeed above the whole human race.'" Five years later, preaching on the same feast day, Luther said, "She was not filled with pride by this praise . . . this immense praise: 'No woman is like unto thee! Thou art more than an empress or a queen . . . blessed above all nobility, wisdom, or saintliness!'"[110]

CRI says, "The title 'Queen' was first used in association with Mary by Pope Martin in the seventh century."[111] This blunder is typical of CRI's level of scholarship. Ephrem the Syrian used the title "Queen" about Mary several times in his *fourth-century* prayers and poems. Here are two of my personal favorites from Ephrem: "Girl, empress and ruler, queen, lady, protect and keep me in your arms, lest Satan, who causes evil, exult over me"[112] and "Queen of all after the Trinity, Consoler after the Paraclete, Mediatrix of the whole world after the Mediator."[113]

CRI's only substantive effort to support its objection to Mary's queenship is a quotation from one Victor Buksbazen: "When Christianity spread throughout the Roman empire . . . Mary replaced the old goddesses. . . . [S]hrines dedicated to Mary began to replace the ancient temples. .

. . Although the tree of paganism was cut down, its roots remained . . . and helped transform Miriam of the Gospel into Mary of popular piety—later into Mariological dogma."[114] Thus, implies CRI, the many pagan earth goddesses, "queens of heaven," became Mary, Queen of heaven.

Buksbazen and CRI here must contend with a more formidable theologian, Karl Barth. Never considered by anyone, Catholic or Protestant, to be a fan of our Lady (he once called Catholic Mariology an "excrescence"), Barth considered the notion that Mariology developed from pagan sources to be ill founded: "It is not to be recommended that we should base our repudiation on the assertion that there has taken place here an irruption from the heathen sphere, an adoption of the idea, current in many non-Christian religions, of a more or less central and original female or mother deity. In dogmatics you can establish everything and nothing from parallels from the history of religions."[115] Supporting Barth, Protestant theologian John de Satgé writes, "It is not necessary to accept . . . . the evil conjunction of Christian piety with the primeval mother-goddess."[116]

The idea that our forefathers in the faith continued to worship their old mother-goddesses under the guise of Mary is simply silly. CRI espouses the common yet unscholarly notion that people of earlier generations were necessarily more stupid than we are today. My readers will know, whether they are scholars or not, that if they consider Mary on the one hand and, let us say, Astarte on the other, they can tell the difference.

Early Christian converts could tell the difference too and perhaps more vividly than we. They had not only lived through their own conversion experience, but doubtless felt in many cases the profound distaste converts sometimes feel for their former religious allegiance. "But they built churches to Mary on the sites of old pagan temples!" one might object. Of course they did. Those pagan temples occupied extremely valuable real estate, and they were often buildings of exceptional beauty. When Christians took possession of them, they were wise enough and shrewd enough to keep them, adapting them to their new needs. They re-consecrated them to the Triune God and often enough added "in honor of Mary."

There was a powerful symbolism at work here too. A lofty temple of Christ, pressing down in all its bulk upon a foundation formerly sacred to a pagan god, crush the site of idolatry—what Christian, seeing such a building, offering Mass in such a building, would not recall the words of God to the ancient serpent, "I will put enmity between you and the woman, and between your offspring and hers; he will *crush* your head, while you strike at his heel" (Gen. 3:15)?

There is another reason why CRI should not open this particular can of worms. If Mary is only the latest in a long line of pagan goddesses, then what about her Son? Rationalists will hasten (*have* hastened) to explain that the risen Christ too is only the latest in a long line of fertility gods, who died and then rose again, symbols of the cycle of vegetation: Osiris, Dionysos, Adonis, many others. If the *Christian Research Journal* ever becomes the learned publication its staffers no doubt wish it to be, they will one day realize that in all Christian history this principle shines clear: Whoever discredits the Mother insults her Son.

8

HYPERDULIA

+

CRI begins the last portion of its attack on Catholic doctrines concerning Mary by claiming that Scripture's words in praise of Mary, "Hail, full of grace, the Lord is with thee" (Luke 1:28) and "Blessed art thou among women and blessed is the fruit of thy womb" (Luke 1:42), do not provide a biblical justification for Catholic devotion to Mary. (These verses, of course, when combined, form the first part of the Hail Mary.) CRI asserts, "The fact that Catholics have utilized these words for the purposes of devotional prayer does not prove they were originally uttered in the same spirit. They need only be taken as declaration of fact; meant to convey special honor, to be sure, but not necessarily 'special veneration.'"[117]

Through twenty centuries the Holy Spirit has been with the Church, as we reflect upon our Scripture and divine Tradition. The Spirit teaches us everything and reminds us of everything Jesus taught (John 14:26). He guides us to all truth (John 16:13). It is quite certain, therefore, that he has brought the Church to a deeper realization of the meanings of Scripture than the original writers enjoyed. Luke 1:28, 42 indeed justifies special veneration of Mary by a deeper realization than Luke had when he wrote his Gospel. But once the Bible is torn from its moorings in the Church, misinterpretations multiply (see Peter 3:16). CRI unwittingly provides many examples of this sad fact.

Another text which blesses Mary is Luke 11:27–28, "'Blessed is the womb that carried you and the breasts at which you nursed.' [Jesus] replied, 'Rather, blessed are those who hear the word of God and keep it.'" CRI says, "That Luke 11:27 would be cited as a proof text for the veneration of Mary is, to the Protestant, striking evidence of a scriptural blindness where Mary is concerned. It should be obvious that, rather than supporting the tendency to venerate Mary, it refutes it."[118] CRI couldn't be more wrong.

Here it will help to look at the Greek particle *menoun* in Luke 11:28, which several translations render as "rather." CRI italicizes this "rather," thus implying (without proof) that Luke is using *menoun* as a particle of contradiction to mean, "No, Mary *isn't* blessed; *rather*, blessed are they, etc." And what is worse, because uncritical and unscholarly, CRI alleges that this interpretation is "obvious." It is far from obvious; it is extremely tenuous and, I believe, quite false.

Margaret E. Thrall, a Protestant scholar, cannot be accused of bias toward the Catholic position. In her study

Greek Particles in the New Testament, suggests the following interpretation of *menoun* in Luke 11:27–28: "What you have said is true as far as it goes. But the blessedness of Mary does not consist simply in the fact of her relationship towards myself, but (*menoun*) in the fact that she shares in the blessedness of those who hear the word of God and keep it, and it is in this that true blessedness lies."[119] I think this is probably the best interpretation of this text, giving the true sense of "rather."

Once again, CRI has shown unawareness of important Protestant testimony. Let's give an illustration of what some other Protestants say. The German Evangelical *Adult Catechism* says, "Mary is not only 'Catholic,' but she is also 'Evangelical.' Protestants tend to forget that. But Mary clearly is the mother of Jesus and closer to him than the closest disciples. With what humanity the New Testament depicts this closeness, without concealing Mary's distance from Jesus! An example of this distance can be seen in Luke (11:27–28), who tells us so much about Mary. . . . Jesus replies, 'Blessed are they who hear the word of God and keep it.' But does that not apply precisely to Mary? She is depicted as exemplary hearer of God's word, as the handmaid of the Lord who says 'Yes' to the will of God, as the blessed one who is nothing of herself but gains everything through God's goodness. Mary is the pattern for men who let themselves be opened and gifted by God, of the community of believers, of the Church."[120]

It is well to be precise here: These German Evangeli-

cals are *not* recommending veneration of Mary. They do
not suggest that one should pray to her. But they do read
Luke 11:27–28 as praise of Mary, not as a snub offered her
by our Lord. And precisely because it is Gospel praise, this
passage provides biblical justification of Catholics' praise
of Christ's Mother.

Now we come to the blunt accusation that Catholics
are sinners and idolaters because of our devotion to
Mary—and to the other saints and the angels. CRI says,
"It was only a matter of time before Mary would be adored
by millions of Catholics around the world. . . . Mary *is*
(and for centuries *has been*) worshiped by millions all over
the world, especially in the Latin countries. . . . Excessive
devotion to Mary in Latin countries and elsewhere in the
Catholic world is not a case of a legitimate practice gone
awry. . . . All *sin* operates according to the same 'give it an
inch and it takes a mile' dynamic—and *idolatry* is sin—
and *religious devotion* to anyone but God is idolatry. This is
the verdict of Scripture."[121]

Before examining Scripture, to refute this charge of
idolatry and sin, I want to take note of the racism evident
in CRI's supercilious reference to the "Latin countries,"
where, it would seem, Catholics are especially prone to
"excessive devotion." John de Satgé—much of whose
work I admire—also mourns "the impression which
Anglo-Saxons gain from visits to Catholic churches during holidays in Latin countries or in Ireland."[122] As CRI
complains of our "excessive devotion," de Satgé winces at
our "debased devotion" in paintings, hymns, and prayers,

which he suggests are "sentimental."[123] But I should like to know what is wrong with sentiment and the sentimental? Surely, the feelings are an important part of the equipment God gives us to live with, to love with, and to pray with. Is not one nation's "sentimentality" another's robust sentiment?

On the whole, I would say that, if Latin sentiment seems treacly sentimentality to you, that is your problem. It is not ours. I believe that Protestantism itself unavoidably shows its Northern European origins. We can respect these, but dourness and a stiff upper lip are simply not our Catholic style. Why should they be? To supercilious and racist remarks about the Catholic Irish and the Catholic peoples of Southern Europe and Latin America, I say, give me a break! Consider for a moment the Orthodox Christians, whose devotion to Mary and the other saints makes our Catholic devotion seem positively Presbyterian!

Catholic and Orthodox theologians make a sharp distinction between *latria* (adoration), the supreme worship rightly given to God alone; *dulia* (veneration and invocation), given to the saints in heaven and to the angels; and *hyperdulia* (special veneration and invocation), offered to Mary, the Mother of God and most exalted of God's creatures. But CRI objects: "While in theory these categories are intended to prevent idolatrous worship of created beings, in practice they have little effect on the religious *feelings* of the masses. How could feelings be subject to such coldly analytical distinctions?"[124]

While I enjoy CRI's Marxist touch here ("the religious

feelings of the masses"), the objection itself has no force, because religious devotion is primarily an exercise of the mind and free will, not of the emotions. Sometimes, devotion *overflows* to the feelings; sometimes it does not. Dryness in prayer, alternating with consolations which overflow to the feelings, is a common experience of those who are constant in prayer, that is, who "pray always" (Luke 18:1), not merely when they feel like it.

The feelings cannot be commanded, whereas our Lord makes the love of God and of our neighbor the object of the two great *commandments* of the Law, and he seats this love not only in the heart and soul, but also in the mind—in fact, in the whole human person of the worshiper. See what Paul writes: "I will pray with the spirit and I will pray with the mind also. I will sing with the spirit and I will sing with the mind also" (1 Cor. 14:15).

We pray to God with our *minds* aware that he is Creator, Redeemer, and Sanctifier, and this awareness is *latria*. We pray to our Lady with our *minds* aware that she is God's noblest and holiest creature, Mother of Jesus and of his Church, and this awareness is *hyperdulia*. We pray to our brothers and sisters, the saints, and to the angels, with our *minds* aware that they are our models, patrons, and intercessors, who offer our prayers to God before the throne of the Lamb (Rev. 4:10, 5:6–14), and this awareness is *dulia*.

It is not necessary for men and women here at prayer explicitly to know these technical terms. It is necessary only to know that God is God and all others are not God.

We Catholics know this; we are in no doubt about it; we know the difference—not because we are particularly bright, but because we are no longer strangers and sojourners, but fellow citizens with the saints and members of the household of God, built upon the foundation of the apostles and prophets, with Jesus Christ himself as the cornerstone (Eph. 2:19–20).

If someone says, "I do not consider Mary, the saints, and the angels to be gods or goddesses, nor do I treat them as such," then he doesn't. You ought to believe him. To insist, in the face of his denial, that he *does* regard these creatures as gods is not only the sin of rash judgment (Luke 6:37, Rom. 14:4, 1 Cor. 4:3–4) and a grave failure in Christian charity, but it is a deficiency in common sense. It is bad use of Scripture, bad theology, bad Church history, and bad manners.

In our theology and practice, we Catholics go with Epiphanius, who wrote, "According to her nature, Mary remains human and feminine. Hence, like other saints, she is unsuited for adoration, though as an elect vessel, she is glorified in a higher degree than others. In like manner, neither Elijah . . . nor John the Baptist . . . nor Thecla may be adored."[125]

De Satgé notes, "What is the place of Mary herself in relation to God? It is that he brought her, as he did all the other children of earth, out of nothing. Although he has since then exalted her to a point of grace immense and inconceivable, nevertheless, in comparison to her Maker, she still remains as nothing. Indeed, she is—far more than any other—*his* creature, because he has wrought more in her than in any other of his creatures. The greater the things he does to her, the more she becomes the work of his hands."[126]

Those who have only a little knowledge easily become pedants and love to correct others who (they rashly judge) know even less than they. But just as the *Imitation of Christ* says, "I would rather feel contrition than know how to define it," so I praise people who love our Lady and express their love with sincere feeling and enthusiasm, even though their vocabulary of praise may be theologically inaccurate. God sees their hearts, and Mary unites them to our Savior, however poorly they express themselves.

Next, what is idolatry? Paul describes it as bartering or exchanging the true, glorious, and immortal God for a lie, paying *latria* (he uses the very word) to a creature rather than to the Creator (Rom. 1:23, 25). Catholics do no such thing. Rather we know and daily experience that the saints, and most of all our Blessed Mother, instruct and edify us by the example of their Christlike lives. Every one of them says to us, as Paul said, "Be imitators of me" (1 Cor. 4:16; see also Phil. 3:17, 1 Thess. 1:6). Like Paul again, the saints and angels are saying to us, "We pray to God that you may not do evil . . . that you may do what is right" (2 Cor. 13:7); "we always pray for you" (2 Thess. 1:11). Our veneration and prayer to Mary and others in heaven redound to the glory of God, whose children we all are. If we neglected to pray to them, we would deny God the glory, praise, and gratitude we owe him for so exalting our brothers and sisters.

But CRI asserts, "*Religious devotion* to anyone but God is idolatry. This is the verdict of Scripture."[127] No, this is the caricature of Scripture. Scripture bids us make every action, every penance and pain, every day, acts of *religious devotion*, fruitful for our own salvation and the salvation of others: "So whether you eat or drink, or whatever else you do, do everything for the glory of God" (1 Cor. 10:31); "Now I rejoice in my sufferings for your sake, and in my flesh I am filling up what is lacking in the afflictions of Christ, on behalf of his Body, which is the Church" (Col. 1:24; see also 2 Cor. 1:3–7).

Romans 13:1–7 teaches us to revere and obey legitimate authority (even the IRS!), because all authority comes from God. Whoever opposes this authority resists God. Thus civic duty and filial piety toward parents, if well understood, are forms of *religious devotion*, commanded by God to be paid to human beings. Indeed, the Lord specified this when he gave Moses the Fourth Commandment—"Honor your father and your mother" (Ex. 20:12).

Psalm 72 is divinely-inspired Scripture. With God's full warranty, therefore, the psalm expresses *religious devotion* (one is tempted here to be wry and to say *excessive devotion*) to a human monarch of Israel. This psalm, of course, is messianic and will find its final fulfillment only in Christ the King, but, in its first and original meaning, it was used in Temple worship as religious devotion to an earthly king.

Jacob, meeting his older brother Esau after a separation of several years, said to him, "To come into your presence is for me like coming into the presence of God!" (Gen. 33:10). (Oh, would that those naughty *Latin Catholics* might behave themselves and use only sober and restrained biblical language as the Patriarch Jacob does!)

To feed, clothe, visit, and shelter the needy are acts of *religious devotion* to God (Matt. 19:16–21, 25:31–36, Gal. 6:2). We are *habitually* to see God in other people. In fact, by percentage, very little of a Christian's time is likely to be spent directly communing with God. We live out our love for God by loving and serving one another (Matt. 25:31–36, Jas. 2:14–17).

But some would protest, "Not in prayer! We mustn't pray to any creature in heaven! God forbid we should ask heavenly dwellers to pray for us or give us anything!" Well, the Patriarch Jacob had a wrestling match with an angel, conversed with him, and *asked him for his blessing* (Gen. 32:23–30). That's prayer to a creature, asking for something. Paul says the Church is Christ's Body. He is eloquent about our need for one another (1 Cor. 12:14–26). We are members of one another (Eph. 4:25).

This family unity is not interrupted by physical death. In fact, Scripture says that baptism is the moment of our true and meaningful death. It is then that we die and are raised to newness of life in Christ (Rom. 6:3–11). "For you have died, and your life is hidden with Christ in God." (Col. 3:3). Physical death is only passage from this world to the next; it does not separate us from the Lord (Rom.

8:38-39). It but marks the moment "when Christ your life appears—then you too will appear with him in glory" (Col. 3:4). We are the Lord's both in this life and in the next (Rom. 14:8), because he is our head and we are his members and members of one another. The Bible famously asks, "Death, where is your victory?" (1 Cor. 15:55). But CRI denies that we can pray to our fellow members of the Mystical Body in heaven. They cannot heed us or take an interest in us or pray for us or in any way serve us. They are bereft of ministry. CRI's false doctrine awards physical death a monumental victory over us, over them, and over Christ. It separates us from our Mother and from our brothers and sisters in Christ, fellow- members whom we need (1 Cor. 12:20, 21, 27).

Baptized members of the Church are called "saints" or "holy ones" in the New Testament. This word (*hagioi* in Greek) is also used of the saints in heaven (Col. 1:12, Eph. 2:19, Rev. 18:20). It represents the Hebrew *qedoshim,* which is used of the saints in heaven in three places in the Old Testament (Zech. 14:5, Ps. 89:6, Dan. 7:22). The saints in heaven, in the persons of the elders in Revelation 5:8, are shown offering to God the prayers of the saints on earth. This activity of the elders is *intercession* by the saints and angels (Rev. 8:3–4) in heaven on behalf of us on earth.

When Christ teaches us to pray, "Thy will be done on earth *as it is in heaven*," he holds up for our imitation the behavior of the saints in heaven, who do his will perfectly. Doing God's will means loving him and loving others as we love ourselves (Matt. 22:36–40). Because the saints are our models of this twofold love, they too must love God and others. What others? Every other human being, no matter who or where, but especially their fellow members of the family of the faith (Gal. 6:10). How can they show their love for us? By caring for our needs. And how can they do this? By praying for us. If they could ignore this love for us, they could not love God nor remain with him in heaven, because the two loves cannot be separated. The Bible says, "This is the commandment we have from him: Whoever loves God must also love his brother" (1 John 4:21); "Bear one anothers' burdens and so you will fulfill the law of Christ" (Gal. 6:2). Scripture cannot be broken—in this world or the next.

The notion that the redeemed in heaven are excused from concern for their brothers and sisters on earth, that they can know nothing of us and do nothing for us, is quite simply indecent. A theology which proposes such selfishness and spiritual paralysis as our heavenly destiny is shameful and unworthy, both of God's love and our human dignity.

CRI asserts that there is no Scriptural basis for believing that Mary and the other saints in heaven can hear prayers offered to them. This assertion violates Luke 16:19–31 and Hebrews 12:1. Revelation 18:20 shows that the saints in heaven would be aware of the destruction of Rome (Babylon) and her empire. Then why would they be unaware, then and now, of the needs, sufferings, prayers, and petitions of their brothers and sisters?

CRI further asks, "Even if [the saints] could hear some

prayers, how could Mary hear *all* of the hundreds of thousands of prayers that undoubtedly are addressed to her every minute of the day? As a creature she, by definition, is limited; she cannot be omniscient and omnipresent!"[128] Here we have what I would call the village atheist's objection—you know, the fellow who can't handle Christ's walking on water or Moses' dividing the Red Sea. God can and does elevate human nature to do what unaided it could not do: "To him who is able to accomplish far more than all we ask or imagine, by the power at work within us, to him be glory in the Church and in Christ Jesus to all generations, forever and ever" (Eph. 3:20).

God empowers Mary and the saints and angels to hear and answer *all* our prayers. It is properly his power, not theirs. By praying to them, we glorify his love and power. The reason we go to them is for his sake alone, to strengthen the bonds of family among ourselves and with him, who has called us all from darkness into his marvelous light. It is not right for anyone, by doubt and unbelief, to earn the rebuke Christ laid upon the Sadducees: "You are misled, because you do not know the Scriptures nor the power of God" (Matt. 22:29).

Catholics believe that "all good giving and every perfect gift is from above, coming down from the Father of lights" (Jas. 1:17). What the saints and angels obtain for us, they obtain from God. Sometimes we hear the suggestion that we should pray not *to* the saints, but only *through* the saints. Some heirs of the Reformation even go so far as to say we should not pray *to* Christ, but only *through* Christ to the Father. If this distinction is meaningful to anyone, let him observe it. It is not meaningful to me.

I prefer to approach a saint directly, as Jacob approached his angelic wrestling partner: "I will not let you go until you bless me!" (Gen. 32:27). Jacob knew that an encounter with heavenly dwellers brings us closer to God: "I have seen God [via his messenger] face to face!" (v. 31). Devotion to the saints and particularly to our Lady increases our awareness of God and our tenderness toward him. This is the common experience of Catholics, and we yearn to share it with all.

CONCLUSION

Hoping to impress its readers with a battery of Scripture texts, CRI concludes that "biblically, all prayer, glory, and devotion belong to God and to his Son, Jesus Christ [and not to Mary and other saints]."[129] I list the objections here with CRI's scriptural texts and with comments:

1. God commands that he alone be worshiped (Luke 4:8).

Both verbs in this text (*latreuein* and *proskynein*) refer to *latria*, the worship due to God alone. It says nothing about *dulia* and *hyperdulia,* which are given to saints and to our Lady. CRI's objection is irrelevant. It begs the question.

2. The apostles refused reverential treatment reserved for God alone (Acts 10:25–26, 14:11–15).

Acts 14:11–15 shows a crowd of pagans attempting to offer an animal sacrifice to Paul and Barnabas, whom they took to be gods. The apostles rightly rejected the "honor," which was idolatrous worship. But 10:25–26 shows a Roman soldier kneeling before Peter to do him homage (*proskynein,* an all-purpose verb, unlike the specific *la-*

treuein, which is not used here.) It would be difficult to prove anything more than fulsome praise on the part of the Roman soldier, which an embarrassed Peter declined out of humility. Neither passage has any bearing upon devotion to our Lady and the saints. In any case, Peter, Paul, and Barnabas were not then in heaven, so these two passages are also irrelevant to our present discussion.

> 3. *Even angels refuse worship; all angels and men are on an equal footing before God (Rev. 22:8–9, 1 Cor. 1:29).*

Notice the straw man CRI sets up: Angels refuse worship, hence men (including dead men in heaven) refuse worship, hence Catholics are wrong to worship the saints. Notice how "worship" is insinuated into the argument? The real issue, which CRI skirts, is whether God's creatures can be honored, not whether they can be worshiped. Let's look at the verses CRI cites.

The author of Revelation, John, reports that he had a kind of fainting spell and later made two prostrations (1:17, 19:10, 22:8–9). In 1:17, he fell at Jesus' feet. Jesus blessed him by touching him with his right hand. In the other two passages, John fell at the feet of an angel who rejects his gesture and tells him to worship God. What is the meaning of these events?

One of the author's purposes in Revelation was to refute gnosticism, a dangerous heresy which taught that matter was hopelessly evil, so that men (partly material because of their bodies) could not hope to be in touch with

God, the utterly pure. But between God and us, the gnostics taught, there are a host of demiurges, neither human nor divine, much less pure than God, but still greater than men. These were identified by "Christian" gnostics with the angels. We should worship these demiurges since it is impossible for us to be in contact with God. Christ was one of these demiurges, the gnostics saying that he was not God and that he had only a phantom body. He was neither man nor God.

John was interested in affirming the divinity of Christ. The fainting fit of 1:17 and the blessing and affirmation of 1:18, taken with the *worship of the Lamb* in 5:6–14, emphasize the divinity of Christ, denying the gnostic doctrine that Christ is a demiurge, neither God nor man. John is teaching us here that we *can* worship God in and through Christ.

John denied we should worship demiurges instead of God, as the gnostics taught. The heresy that angels and Christ are demiurges and are to be worshiped as such is rejected. Rather, angels are angels and do not receive worship. Christ is both man and God and does receive worship. The three texts do not deal with and have no bearing upon our love of and friendship with our Lady and the other saints and angels.

The other verse used by CRI is 1 Corinthians 1:29 and is used to illustrate this statement: "Even angels emphatically refuse worship, insisting that all angels and men are on an equal footing of humility before God."[130] But the text has nothing to say about angels at all nor about anybody's "equal footing." Verse 29 needs to be read in its context (1:26–31), as all Scripture does.

The passage is about our calling, by which God "called [us] out of darkness into his wonderful light" (1 Pet. 2:9). This calling does not depend upon any natural endowments of ours, upon worldly wisdom or prestige or nobility of birth. Quite the contrary—God has called the foolish and the weak and the lowly. Why? So that it may be evident that our being in Christ is entirely God's doing. As a result, Christ is free to endow us with his own "wisdom from God, as well as righteousness, sanctification, and redemption" (1 Cor. 1:30). Although no flesh (no mere human being prior to his calling in Christ) may boast before God (v. 29) because of purely human (v. 26, "fleshly" in Greek) endowments, we must boast in (what we have received from) the Lord (v. 31).

The saints in heaven must boast in the Lord more than any of us, because they are the people of the ten golden coins, who have worked to gain ten more (Luke 19:16–17). They have proved themselves good soil, which from the sowing of the Word produces a hundredfold harvest (Mark 4:8, 20). 1 Corinthians 1:29–31 is, in fact, a foundation text which validates our special regard (*dulia* and *hyperdulia*) for the saints and Mary, God's special friends and his Mother.

> 4. God "makes it clear that no created being will glory before him—he will share his glory with no one" (Is. 42:8).[131]

The text from Isaiah reads: "I am the Lord, this is my name; my glory I give to no other, nor my praise to idols." God will not tolerate competition—he is the only God. Isaiah 42:8 is a rejection of polytheism, which would make the God of Israel only one figure in a vast pantheon.

But is it "clear," as CRI asserts, that God will share his glory with no one? To be sure, there is a divine glory which is the very essence of God, which is himself, that he can share with no created being. Nobody but God can be God. But, in a limited way, God does share his glory by sharing his nature with his adopted children, the brothers and sisters of his firstborn Son (Rom. 8:29). This is the teaching of 2 Peter 1:3–4: "His divine power has bestowed on us everything that makes for life and devotion, through the knowledge of him who called us by his own glory and power. Through these he has bestowed on us the precious and very great promises, so that through them you may come to share in the divine nature." This sharing in God's nature makes us a new creation (2 Cor. 5:17).

Scripture teaches that God bestows this glory of his on his children: "For a sun and a shield is the Lord God; grace and glory he bestows" (Ps. 84:12); "Then Jerusalem shall be my joy, my praise, my glory" (Jer. 33:9); "I will put my salvation within Zion, and give my glory to Israel." (Is. 46:13) Christ's Church, therefore, receives his salvation and glory, because the Church is the new Jerusalem, the new Israel (Gal. 6:16; Rev. 21:2, 21:12, 3:12).

We are now in glory, and we are destined for glory. The texts which witness to this are so numerous, I shall list only some in a footnote,[132] so as not to delay the reader here. But I would say to anyone who thinks that God is not going to share his glory with us, his children, his saints, well, as Eliza Doolittle sings, "Just you wite!" God's whole plan of salvation involves his sharing his glory with his redeemed and adopted children.

We praise and venerate the saints in heaven, praying to them, praying with them to the Father through Christ in the Spirit, thanking God who prepares us to share in the inheritance of the saints in light (Col. 1:12). Our devotion to Mary, God's Mother and ours, and to our brothers and sisters, the saints, is all the more solid, humble, and grateful because we know that even the holiest and most fervent Christians on earth cannot possibly honor them as much as God has already honored them.

CRI finally returns to the charge that devotion to Mary and the other saints somehow diminishes Christ. Neither the Bible nor twenty centuries of Christian experience uphold that accusation. Not only do Mary and the saints receive all they have from Christ, but Christ is no miser. Whatever we see him doing, we see him associating his members in his work.

He is our unique judge (John 5:22, 27, 2 Tim. 4:1, Jas. 4:12, 1 Pet. 4:5), but Scripture teaches that Christ's disciples will share his work of judgment (Matt. 19:28; 1 Cor. 6:2-3). He is the Church's one foundation (1 Cor. 3:11), but Christ shares this dignity with Peter (Matt. 16:18) and with the apostles and prophets (Eph. 2:19-20, Rev. 21:14). Christ is our King (Dan. 7:13-14), but his disciples will rule with him (7:27). He does not diminish his kingly power by sharing it; rather, he manifests it to God's glory. Christ is our High Priest, offering himself, the Lamb of God, as the one perfect sacrifice for sins (Heb. 2:17, 3:1, 4:14ff., 5:8–10, 7:26ff., 8:1, 9:11–28). Yet we share his priesthood, offering spiritual sacrifices in union with him (Rom. 12:1, 15:16; Heb. 13:15–16; 1 Pet. 2:5-9; Rev. 1:6, 5:10, 20:6). Our sharing in his priesthood does not diminish him. Indeed, we have become his partners (Heb. 3:14).

We are taught that every member of Christ's Body needs every other member (1 Cor. 12:12–26). The pity is that for the past five hundred years, some Christians have been saying to Mary and the other saints in heaven, "We don't need you, and we don't want you." Any way you slice that, it is unbiblical and it is wrong.

A Mexican-American girl, a senior at the university where I work, last year traveled around Europe by train. She kept in her backpack a copy of *The Story of a Soul,* the autobiography of Therese of Lisieux, given her by one of her boyfriends. In her journal of the trip she wrote these words about the effect the saint had on her: "What a beautiful saint! I love her. Sometimes in reading about her relationship with God, I could really relate. I know that I love God more than fear him, because I know he loves me. When Therese said that sometimes she felt like a little child who just wanted to hide her face in the embrace of Jesus, my soul leaped. I feel like that so often, especially now that I'm traveling on my own. But Therese has given me strength in knowing that God will always guide me and protect me because he loves me as his own little girl—much more than my parents could ever love me—and that's so much that I can't even conceive it. It makes me so happy to think about it, though, that I just feel my chest getting heavy and my eyes fill with tears of joy. I love God."

This young woman, just one generation away from Mexico, knows what many millions of Catholics everywhere have known for twenty centuries: Our Lady and the saints bring us more powerfully and more surely to God and to Jesus our Savior than we could come without their aid. That is their divine calling in heaven. God works through them, and most of all through Mary.

We are never left on our own. They are members with us of Christ's Body, the Church, ready to help us, whether we know them or not but especially ready when we are aware of them and call on them for help. "Therefore, since we are surrounded by so great a cloud of witnesses, let us rid ourselves of every burden and sin that clings to us, and persevere in running the race that lies before us while keeping our eyes fixed on Jesus, the leader and perfecter of faith" (Heb. 12:1–2).

I reassure anyone who cares: Devotion to Mary brings us closer to Christ and does the job more quickly than ignoring her does. As Luther once said (on another subject, but I love his style): "If you do not want to believe it, then don't. The loss will be yours."[133]

NOTES

[1] Elliott Miller, "The Mary of Roman Catholicism," *Christian Research Journal*, Summer 1990, 10. The second part of Miller's article appeared in the Fall 1990 issue. In these notes the two parts are referred to as Part 1 and Part 2.

[2] Part 2, 31, 32.

[3] Part 1, 10.

[4] K. E. Skydsgaard, *One in Christ, Protestant and Catholic* (Philadelphia: Muhlenberg, 1957), quoted in Bernard Leeming, "Protestants and Our Lady," *Marian Library Studies*, nos. 128/129, Jan./Feb. 1967, 17.

[5] Quoted in Albert J. Nevins, *Answering a Fundamentalist* (Huntington: Our Sunday Visitor), 97.

[6] Part 1, 10-11.

[7] Joseph Gallegos, Message 352, Message Base 4, "Ask Father" conference, Catholic Information Network echo, Mar. 1, 1991.

[8] Part 1, 11.

[9] John de Satgé, *Down to Earth: The New Protestant Vision of the Virgin Mary* (Consortium, 1976), 52.

[10] Jaroslav Pelikan, ed., *Luther's Works* (St. Louis: Concordia), 24:107.

[11] Part 1, 11.

[12] Quoted in Max Thurian, *Mary, Mother of All Christians* (New York: Herder and Herder, 1964), 89. Thurian is a convert to Catholicism.

[13] Ibid.

[14] Part 1, 11.

[15] *Luther's Works*, 22:492–493.

[16] Part 1, 11.

[17] Ibid., 12.

[18] *Our Jesuit Life* (St. Louis: Institute of Jesuit Sources, 1990), II, IV, A, 33.

[19] Thurian, 24.

[20] Matthew 10:38, 19:21, Romans 8:16–17, Philippians 1:28–29, Colossians 1:24, Hebrews 12:11, 1 Peter 2:19–21.

[21] Part 1, 15.

[22] Ibid., 12.

[23] Ibid., 15.

[24] Karl Keating, *Catholicism and Fundamentalism: The Attack on "Romanism" by "Bible Christians"* (San Francisco: Ignatius, 1988), 282–289.

[25] The Septuagint is a Greek translation of the Hebrew Bible, produced in the third century B.C. in Egypt.

[26] Part 1, 12.

[27] Ibid.

[28] Ibid.

[29] David Hill, *Greek Words and Hebrew Meanings* (Cambridge: Cambridge University Press, 1967), 16–18.

[30] Part 1, 13.

[31] Ibid.

[32] Augustine, *Holy Virginity*, 4, 4.

[33] *Luther's Works*, vol. 22, 23 (emphasis added).

[34] Quoted in Leeming, 9.

[35] Ibid.

[36] Augustin Bea, "Mary and the Protestants," *Marian Studies* 83, April 1961, 1 (emphasis added).

[37] De Satgé, 112–113.

[38] *Ineffabilis Deus* (1854).

[39] Part 1, 14.

[40] Karl Keating, *Catholicism and Fundamentalism* (San Francisco: Ignatius Press, 1988), 269.

[41] Part 1, 14.

[42] Ibid.

[43] H. W. Smyth, *Greek Grammar* (Cambridge: Harvard University Press, 1968), 108-109.

[44] Blass and DeBrunner, *Greek Grammar of the New Testament* (Chicago: University of Chicago Press, 1961), 166.

[45] Smyth, sec. 1852:c:1.

[46] Ibid., sec. 1852:c, note.

[47] Blass and DeBrunner, 175.

[48] Smyth, sec. 1852:b.

[49] The next three examples are taken from Blass and DeBrunner, 175–176.

[50] Jaroslav Pelikan, ed., *Luther's Works* (St. Louis: Concordia), vol. 43, 40.

[51] Max Thurian, *Mary, Mother of All Christians* (New York: Herder and Herder, 1964), 197.

[52] Part 1, 14.

[53] Ibid.

[54] Thurian, 21.

[55] Part 1, 14.

[56] The texts are Ecclesiastes 7:20, Galatians 3:22, Romans 3:23, 5:12, 11:32.

[57] John de Satgé, *Down to Earth: The New Protestant Vision of the Virgin Mary* (Consortium, 1976), 73.

[58] *Munificentissimus Deus*, 44.

[59] Lawrence P. Everett, "Mary's Death and Bodily Assumption" in J. Carol, *Mariology*, vol. 2, 461.

[60] *Lumen Gentium*, 65.

[61] M.-J. Nicholas, "Protestants, Catholics, and Mary," *Marian Studies* 90 (March 1962), 7.

[62] Part 1, 14., quoting Victor Buksbazen, *Miriam, the Virgin of Nazareth* (Philadelphia: Spearhead Press, 1963), 196.

[63] Part 1, 15, quoting Karl Rahner, *Mary, Mother of the Lord* (London: Anthony Clarke Books, 1963), 16.

[64] Part 1, 15.

[65] Everett, 483.

[66] Thomas Mozley, *Reminiscences of Oriel College and the Oxford Movement* (London: Farnborough, Gregg, 1969), vol. 2, 368.

[67] J. Carol, *Mariology*, vol. 2, 145–146.

[68] Part 1, 15.

[69] Everett, 475.

[70] Cyril Vollert, *A Theology of Mary* (New York: Herder and Herder, 1965), 233–234.

[71] Martin Marty of the University of Chicago Divinity School gives this number in *U.S. News and World Report*, March 4, 1991, 51.

[72] Vollert, 227–228.

[73] Part 1, 15.

[74] F. J. Sheed, *Theology for Beginners* (Ann Arbor: Servant, 1981), 131–132.

[75] Part 2, 28.

[76] *Luther's Works* (Weimar), 10:71:19–73:2.

[77] Ibid, 11:224:8.

[78] Ibid.

[79] Ibid., 29:655:26–656:7.

[80] John de Satgé, *Down to Earth: The New Protestant Vision of the Virgin Mary* (Consortium, 1976), 111. The title of de Satgé's fourth chapter is "Mary, Mother of Her Son's People."

[81] Nicolas Zernov, *Eastern Christendom* (London: Weidenfeld and Nicolean, 1961), 279.

[82] John Paul II, *Redemptoris Mater*, note 130.

[83] Part 2, 28.

[84] Ludwig Ott, *Fundamentals of Catholic Dogma* (Rockford: TAN Books, 1974), 212.

[85] Part 2, 29.

[86] *Luther's Works,* 31:273.

[87] John de Satgé, *Down to Earth: The New Protestant Vision of the Virgin Mary* (Consortium, 1976), 52.

[88] Quoted by de Satgé, ibid., 62.

[89] James O'Mahony, quoted in *The Official Handbook of the Legion of Mary* (Dublin: Concilium Legionis Mariae, 1969), 9.

[90] Part 2, 29.

[91] Ibid.

[92] Ibid., 30.

[93] Ibid.

[94] Ibid. This notion of a line is a metaphor nowhere used in Scripture or in Catholic theology.

[95] Ibid., 30–31.

[96] Ibid., 30.

[97] CRI's arguments against the Catholic doctrine of the communion of saints are refuted in Patrick Madrid, "Any Friend of God's Is a Friend of Mine," *This Rock*, September 1992, 7–13.

[98] Ibid.

[99] Ibid.

[100] Ibid.

[101] Ibid.

[102] Ibid., 30.

[103] Ibid.

[104] See also Matthew 7:21–23, 19:16–17, 25:34–36; Luke 6:27–36, 46–49; Acts 10:35; Rom. 2:6, 13; Gal. 5:4–6; Col. 3:23; Phil. 2:12–13; Heb. 10:24; Jas. 1:22–25, 2:14–26; 1 John 3:7, 19–24, 5:3.

[105] Ibid., quoting Vatican II's *Dogmatic Constitution on the Church (Lumen Gentium)*, 62. See also Ambrose, *Letters* 63, PL 16:1218.

[106] Pius XII, *Ad Caeli Reginam*, no. 25, in *Four Marian Encyclicals*, ed. E. R. Lawlor (New York: Paulist Press, 1959), 104.

[107] All these texts from Eastern liturgies are found in Cuthbert Gumbinger, "Mary in the Eastern Liturgies," in J. Carol, *Mariology*, 1:185–244.

[108] Christopher O'Donnell, *Life in the Spirit and Mary* (Wilmington: Glazier, 1981), 45.

[109] *Luther's Works*, 21:327.

[110] Ibid., 36:208, 45:107.

[111] Part 2, 31.

[112] Ephrem, *"Oratrio ad SS. Dei Matrem,"* *Opera Omnia*, ed. Assemani, t. III (Rome, 1747), 546.

[113] J. Carol, 1:232.

[114] Part 2, 32.

[115] Karl Barth, *Church Dogmatics* (Edinburgh: T & T Clark, 1936-1960), 1:143.

[116] John de Satgé, *Down to Earth: The New Protestant Vision of the Virgin Mary* (Consortium, 1976), 80.

[117] Part 2, 32. CRI here implicitly espouses, without proof, the narrowly Fundamentalist view that Scripture ought to be read only according to the literal meaning of the original authors. Yet Scripture itself gives examples of drawing enriched meanings from earlier texts, whose authors were not explicitly aware of those meanings.

[118] Ibid.

[119] Margaret E. Thrall, *Greek Particles in the New Testament* (Grand Rapids: Eerdmans, 1962), 35.

[120] Quoted in Albert J. Nevins, *Answering a Fundamentalist* (Huntington: Our Sunday Visitor, 1990), 97–98.

[121] Part 2, 31–32.

[122] John de Satgé, *Down to Earth: The New Protestant Vision of the Virgin Mary* (Consortium, 1976), 117.

[123] Ibid., 111.

[124] Part 2, 32.

[125] Epiphanius, *Panarion, Haer.* 79, no. 5, *Patres Graeci,* XLII, 47.

[126] De Satgé, 117.

[127] Part 2, 32.

[128] Part 2, 33.

[129] Ibid.

[130] Ibid.

[131] Ibid.

[132] Romans 2:6–7, 10, 8:18; 1 Cor. 2:7, 2 Cor. 3:18, 4:17, Col. 1:27, 3:1–4, 1 Thess. 2:12, 2 Thess. 2:14, 2 Tim. 2:10, Heb. 2:9–10, 1 Pet. 1:7, 5:4.

[133] *Luther's Works*, 23:83.

Cut Through the Confusion

Does it bother you when the Holy Sacrifice of the Mass gets turned into a platform for radical liberal or feminist propaganda?

Perhaps you're tired of liturgical dancers prancing around the altar during Mass . . . or lectors changing the words of Sacred Scripture to eliminate male references . . . or the priest changing the words of consecration to suit his own theological ideas.

If you've seen or heard about these or many other liturgical abuses—and you'd like to know what you can do to help protect the sacred dignity of the Mass—then you're going to love *Mass Confusion: The Do's and Don'ts of Catholic Worship.*

"A timely and useful book . . . Essential reading for any faithful Catholic who wishes to vindicate his right to true and proper worship."

— Charles Wilson, Executive Director, The St. Joseph Foundation

CLEAR, CONCISE ANSWERS

Written by James Akin—a leading religion writer, Catholic apologist, and contributing editor to *This Rock* magazine—*Mass Confusion* is fast becoming a well-respected source of clear, concise answers about today's most common questions concerning the liturgy (especially liturgical abuses).

SUFFER NO LONGER!

You'll love *Mass Confusion* because it makes liturgical issues understandable for the laity. The faithful need to realize that the liturgy is not the exclusive domain of liturgical "experts." It belongs to the whole People of God.

MASS CONFUSION TO THE RESCUE!

Mass Confusion empowers priests and laity alike to deal with the "liturgical elite." It explains what the Church does and doesn't allow in the liturgy. It gives you answers to your questions on hundreds of liturgical issues, distilled from a mountain of liturgical documents. It silences personal "interpretation" of the Church's liturgical law. And it documents your right to have Mass celebrated as the Church intended.

Best of all, it provides all this information in a clear and concise way. You'll love the special "Answers At-A-Glance" appendix that quickly covers the most commonly asked questions about liturgical practices. For example:

▲▲▲

What are the proper times to stand, sit, or kneel?
How much liberty does a priest have with the words of the Mass?
Where does the tabernacle go, and should there even be one?
Can the priest prohibit you from kneeling to receive Communion?
Can Communion be given to Protestants at weddings and funerals?
Is it okay to use baskets to hold consecrated Hosts?
May an image of the resurrected Christ be used in place of a cross?

▼▼▼

After reading *Mass Confusion*, you'll see why it's an indispensable handbook for Catholics who love the Mass and who are loyal to the Magisterium of the Church.

ACT NOW!

To obtain your copy for only $15.95 (US) plus S & H, simply call **TOLL FREE 1-888-291-8000** with your credit card order.

How To Easily Answer And Refute Every Attack Upon The Catholic Faith!

When someone attacks the Catholic faith, do you know how to answer them?

Every day, Protestant Fundamentalists and Evangelicals, Jehovah's Witnesses, Mormons, Seventh Day Adventists, unbelievers, and many others launch massive attacks upon the Catholic faith.

But if you don't know how to answer and refute their attacks, many good people will be kept from knowing the truth.

Every attack upon the Catholic faith has a solid answer that takes just a few minutes to learn and explain to others. And once you discover these answers, your own faith will be strengthened—and you'll be able to have a positive impact on the lives of many other people as you share your faith with them!

Where Should You Go To Get Solid Answers?

Just subscribe to *This Rock*—today's most effective Catholic apologetics magazine. *This Rock* is published by Catholic Answers—the country's largest lay-run apostolate dedicated to Catholic apologetics and evangelization.

This Rock magazine teaches you how to gently and charitably explain Catholic beliefs —and how to overcome the many misconceptions held by non-Catholics about the Catholic faith.

What Do You Get When You Read THIS ROCK?

Each issue is 48 pages long—chock full of meaty articles that really help you understand your Catholic faith and share it with others. For instance . . .

✛ You'll be enlightened by our Interviews with today's top Catholic leaders.

✛ You'll marvel at "The Fathers Know Best"—where we give you proofs from writings of the earliest Christians that the early Church was Catholic.

✛ You'll find our "Quick Questions" section to be very helpful.

✛ You'll be uplifted by our "Conversion Stories" section.

✛ Drawing on sources from web sites to magazines, "Dragnet" offers insightful commentary on the latest issues having to do with Catholic—and anti-Catholic—thought.

Plus, each issue contains so many fascinating articles—and light-hearted humor sprinkled throughout—you'll find it hard to put down!

Listen to What Some Of Our Readers Say

"I love your magazine and what it teaches! I'm a United Methodist pastor who is seriously looking at the Catholic Church, and This Rock provides me with many of the answers I've been looking for." —Jeff F., Clarksville, TN

"As a convert to Catholicism, I am often faced with the opportunity to defend my faith. This Rock has been a valuable asset in that effort." —Cynthia C., Roanoke, VA

"My knowledge of the Catholic faith has advanced by leaps and bounds just through reading your magazine." —Colleen C., Lynchburg, VA

Now You Can Sample It . . .FREE!

Just call us toll free at 1-888-291-8000

We'll send you three months of *This Rock* absolutely FREE—so you can see for yourself why this is one magazine you definitely should be reading each and every month. Call to get your FREE 3-month trial subscription started TODAY!

Subscription rates for the U.S. are $39.95 for one year and $71.95 for two years. Please call for rates outside the U.S.